CULTURAL ACTIVITIES SERI

T·O·L·I

CHICKASAW STICKBALL THEN AND NOW

STANLEY NELSON

To the players, coaches, and leaders
of Chikasha Toli and Chikasha Bak Bak

CONTENTS

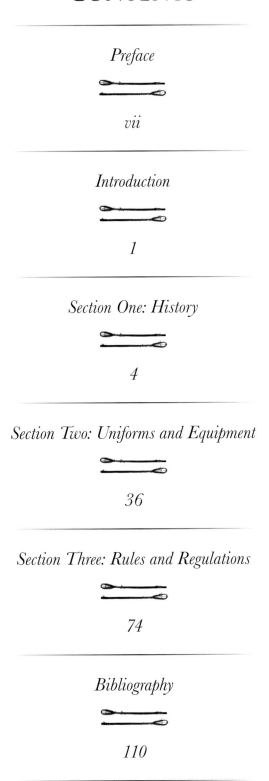

PREFACE

We pack a toolkit of assumptions on each journey of discovery we take, especially when we set out to investigate the past. As a sailor regards a sextant or spyglass, an explorer considers a compass, and a cartographer esteems the curious instruments of the craft, we deem our assumptions are necessary, even fundamental, as if they might somehow contain the true, or at least the best accepted, means not only to find what we seek, but also to validate it. However, the cultural explorer—whether a veteran historian, a trained anthropologist, a learned linguist, or a mere pedestrian writer whose curiosity tends to pull him into odd, ephemeral turnouts while all authoritative signs point along well-marked paths to elsewhere—should bear in mind that our assumptions, handy as they seem, are merely that. They can help you to get where you want to go, but cannot explain everything you find. And they cannot reveal what is no longer "there," in the most broadly understood sense of the term.

So they are little help when it comes to the search for stickball's past, particularly if we pursue the idea of reconstructing its story. That journey takes us into a counter-intuitive realm where we encounter much more mystery than history. It hardly helps that we are also surrounded by the disruptive and often impertinent intrusions of the outlandish, turbulent carnival of modern sports, even while the trail of stickball—to'li'—leads us ultimately so far from them, we begin to intuit a great deal more basis for distinction than comparison.

The available artifacts, kept and catalogued like so many bones in museums and collections, only suggest the durable imprint of to'li' among Chickasaws as a cultural custom. The technically sparse accounts set down by invader observers of the contact period—who were perhaps less interested in what could be learned about Natives than in what could be done with or to them—merely tantalize the predominant culture's ironic preference for documentation. To document such evidence is to bless it with the exalted status of "provenance," which is insisted upon as a conclusive talisman of authenticity, the price of admission to a peculiar, rarefied status of consideration as original and historical, as opposed to ambiguous and speculative.

Oddly, the invaders of the so-called New World considered themselves equal to the tasks of discovering, establishing or synthesizing provenance. For the latter, they always could use categorization, one of their most dependable tools of assumption. And it was simple to use. To'li' only had to pass the look-alike, smell-alike, and sound-alike tests they used like sieves to deduce similarities between their games back in the aptly named Old World, so as to catalogue them together, as they seemed to prefer. In that manner they forged a cold, iron link from to'li' to a northern Iroquoian game they would pointedly expropriate and give the European name, "lacrosse." After all, the Iroquois game was the first they saw after they landed, and the invaders tended to go with what they were most familiar and therefore comfortable with. Meanwhile, whispers from the humid deeps of the Southeastern forests insinuated that they had never found the trail of to'li', and had perhaps lost it for good.

Chickasaws only shrug at all that. For us, to'li' needs no credentials, and certainly no introduction, any more than our own skins, even after the length of time while its most traditional practices "went to sleep," as some say, or after many of its past rituals have submerged into the wake of time. To Chickasaws, to'li' is less about history or fact or authenticity, even if we might acknowledge such things, than a fundamental matter of being who we are and doing what we do. It is not only a game. It is our game.

To'li' arises fully grown from our identification as Chickasaws. In short, the game does not make us who we are. Rather, we make stickball Chickasaw—as much so today as ever it was, even while we apply quiet study to its rebuilding, and sometimes modify it to fit our culture as it stands, and while it changes. Therefore, the spectator at any modern Chickasaw stickball game can be assured that what is seen on the field, even as it might change over time, is and will be authentic, regardless and even in defiance of what others might believe, theorize, or insist.

The side paths that led to the realizations detailed above, among others, were learned and put to invaluable use along the trail of Chikasha to'li'. Each were found among the prints of the giants whose steps this plodding writer followed.

Lokosh (Joshua D. Hinson) is roundly recognized not only as a leader in the Chickasaw Nation's revitalization of the people's language, but also as a seasoned and learned researcher and player of to'li'. Upon his earlier written works this title depends in great part, and whatever courage is applied herein finds its strength in his arguments for taking the cultural risk of insistence on an honest, originally Native perspective toward America's shared history.

Amanda J. Cobb-Greetham is perhaps better known by the people of the Nation for her accomplishments as a leader and ambassador among them before she ascended to a well-deserved position of academic honor, and has earned acknowledgment as a leading Native scholar and professor. At all times, she has lent forceful logic and incisive observation to the case for fundamental change in the study of Native and especially Chickasaw history and culture.

John Dyson, retired in title only as a professor, stands apart as a linguist extraordinaire whose intuitive research into the Chickasaw language, in particular, has coaxed out a resonant and at times echoing voice from the past, often out of corners where archaeology and textual criticism tend to find only silence.

Phillip Carroll Morgan, a friend who it is a privilege to count as a partner in Native literary crime, is the one who, for this writer, kicked down the door and led the way out of the temple of the invaders' rather ossified version of our shared history. His seminal and revolutionary work, *Riding Out the Storm: Nineteenth Century Chickasaw Governors, Their Lives and Intellectual Legacy*, rises to premier significance in that regard.

Even more pertinent to the subject of this title are the invaluable counsels, examples, and guidance of the leaders and players involved in the present renaissance of Chikasha to'li'. Clovis Hamilton, Ric Greenwood, Brad Greenwood, Brandon White Eagle, Wakeah Vigil, Andrea Mann, Brittany Wood, Amber Fox, and Jeremy Wallace are but a few of this diligent legion led by Lisa John, current secretary of the Nation's Department of Culture and Humanities, and Lori Hamilton, executive officer of the Chickasaw Nation's Division of History and Culture.

Governor Bill Anoatubby, the leader of the Chickasaw Nation whose role in our cultural renaissance cannot be overstated, has been invaluable for his support of Chikasha to'li', a concern intuitively linked to his keen interest in the revival of Chickasaw stomp dancing and the formation and perpetuation of the Chickasaw Nation Dance Troupe. Because of his leadership the two immensely important cultural programs found strength to begin, and today continue to honor Chickasaw ancestors, and to preserve Chickasaw traditions and perpetuate Chickasaw history and culture for future generations.

To all the above every success this work might enjoy is owed, and none of its writer's failures may be laid against them.

INTRODUCTION

Accounts of to'li' set down by European observers of the eighteenth and nineteenth centuries offer few of the technical details that interest modern fanciers of mass-marketed pastimes. They do describe as much of the game's attendant pageantry and ceremony as the Southeastern people would allow outsiders to see. The Chickasaws—and the Cherokees, Creeks, Seminoles, and Choctaws—would not let the invaders witness all their traditional purifications, preparations, and rituals before and after the games, although they didn't mind sharing descriptions of them. And even if the invaders of the Native world might have appreciated the strategic and even cultural reasons for such exclusivity, the game itself posed and remained a puzzle. It defied their curiosity, which tended to focus on technique.

Mostly for that reason, the apparently tight-lipped, forbidding culture of to'li' also tantalized the European tendency toward comparison and its favorite cousin, categorization. On one hand, it looked enough like their auld field sports of cricket, hurley, caid, and the game of football the British colonists would, after a time, call "soccer." On the other, it stood to itself, aloof and mercurial.

The European invaders esteemed themselves much too clever to accept matters as they appeared. They seized upon a cultural statement discerned within the translation of a nickname for the game as it was shared among Southeastern peoples: "little brother of war." So there it was, from the invaders' perspective, at least: a handy and familiar niche for to'li', easy to unpack and rationalize. As a bonus, it lay but a short conceptual step from their popular, if ill-considered, trope of the reflexively warlike Native. The result was inevitable to anyone familiar with European cultural philosophy. Somewhat like scientists who theorize the entirety of a dinosaur from a mere fragment of fossil, the invaders turned the nickname into a characterization they could feel comfortable with, neatly grafted into their concepts and codes of warfare—chivalry, abandon, discipline, sacrifice, ritual, and above all, their ideal of teamwork. The colors of stickball equipment and regalia, for which Chickasaws often chose red and black—the hues of honor and warfare—were herded into neat categories, next to the common assumptions about inspirations for colors and designs found on the uniforms of organized teams of the invaders' popular sports, with their stylized messages of identification and intimidation. The invaders, who liked to close concepts within boundaries, encased the glib comparisons with reductionism—e.g., don't trouble with thinking past what seems to work.

But Chickasaw to'li' and Chickasaw warfare would not play inside the invaders' lines. Non-Natives favored all-or-nothing endeavors, with decisive conquest at stake—an ironic preference, given their metastasizing cycles of seasonal sports. In the case of war, they failed to examine how and why Chickasaws regarded it from a different, even if gravely considered, cultural perspective.

To the Europeans, the Chickasaw way of waging war, which seldom leaned toward annihilation and conclusive subjugation, as theirs did, seemed worse than puzzling or inscrutable. In practical situations, it triggered the invaders' reflex to regard such disagreement as insolence or worse, ignorance, as if the Chickasaws just didn't get the point, although they recognized with esteem our deep experience and background in warfare. But for the Europeans to appreciate the full measure of our warriors' approach would have required greater attention to to'li' and assiduous study of its fundamental importance to Southeastern and Chickasaw culture. However, the invaders' consistent, if flexible, ideas about progress, conquest, and manifest destiny tended to exclude any strategy that smacked of cultural concession.

Here at last is what the invaders missed in their blinding rush toward acquisitive colonization: that from rituals of preparation to the aftermath of anticipation for the next clash, the Chickasaws' ways of warfare and to'li' reflect each other, and in turn, the indomitable soul of our people. The little brother of war, as one of our own, is not much smaller, hardly younger, and every bit the same flesh and blood. And Chickasaws keep to'li' close, within the family, an unconquered and unconquerable part of who we are.

HISTORY

A characteristic European-style depiction of Hernando de Soto's putative discovery of the Mississippi River as portrayed in 1853 by artist William Henry Powell. The work is placed in the Rotunda of the U.S. Capitol building, and has appeared on printed banknotes and bills. In it, de Soto, astride a mighty white horse, occupies the prime visual space, entering while flanked in force by a coterie of Spaniard clerics, cavaliers and battle-seasoned troops. Natives, depicted as living in Plains-style teepees, cower and kowtow with deferential fear and respect.

By William Henry Powell, *Discovery of the Mississippi by De Soto*, Architect of the Capitol, Washington, D.C.

Throughout the so-called contact period, Chicka-saw warriors were roundly counted among the most feared on the continent, beheld with dread by all, and especially by their enemies. Those enemies in-cluded, for an instructive example, the battalion of avari-cious sixteenth-century Spaniards led by Hernando de Soto. The Chickasaws summarily ruined de Soto's force and put it to flight, although the longest pedantic traditions of American history routinely consider him and his cohort as technologically, technically, and culturally superior. It remains a problem, then, to realize how our tribe achieved such victory against the Spaniards. To this day settler historians persist, if desperately, at casting the Chickasaws' attacks as clever forays by which we hoped to prod the irresistible European invaders out of our vulnerable territory.

An objective survey of the matter develops an oppo-site picture. Various accounts establish that our ancestors in the Chickasaw Homeland clearly instructed the Span-iards to expect grim consequences should they insist on crossing the Tombigbee River to enter our territory. Still, de Soto and his troops pressed on, either impelled by practical urgency or perhaps assuming the "Chicaza," as they mis-named the Natives who faced them from across the water, would be hard pressed to prevent them. The Spaniards' decision would prove fateful, although one might think dif-ferently if persuaded by the baffling, often counter-intuitive, and transparently slanted accounts spun by the pens of de Soto's so-called chroniclers.

The circumspect observer instead sees that from the beginning, the Chicaza commanded firm control of every situation. Moreover, everything we did concern-ing the Spaniards followed strictly our immemorial tradi-tions of diplomacy, warfare, and to'li'. The Chicaza offered a challenge, and the Oshpaani', as the ancestors' tongue would render their name, accepted, even if unwittingly.

The Chicaza took account of the opponents' disposition, determined them taxed by travel and travail, and so gave them generous time and space to rest and prepare, not to mention provisions to restore and sustain them in the meantime. Those things were not at all provided out of awe or fear—even if we might have made it seem so—but because we could. At least as importantly, that also kept with our standards of fair play in the case of war, or its little brother, to'li'. And we thereby demonstrated a characteristic touch for ironic gamesmanship. Whether the Spaniards intuited such nuances or recognized any of it as a signal of an approaching confrontation—and one should allow they might have—hardly posed a concern for our Chicaza.

The first nighttime attack began abruptly, as does a game of to'li'. It is said the encamped Spaniard force amounted to between four and five hundred, although a few circumstances raise questions about that number, or at least whether so many were able to bear arms. One is that—according to the "chroniclers"—an earlier, reportedly ruinous ambush by a confederated army of Natives at the fortress of Mabila, some distance to the east in what is now Alabama, had left de Soto with about four hundred out of his original six hundred and twenty men, and of that remainder more than a hundred still bore wounds. Another is that the watch on the night of the Chicaza's first attack, even given the chroniclers' assertion that de Soto himself had warned his men to imitate his vigilance and preparedness, was reported to be only three mounted troops, an oddly small number to handle guard duty over a force of battalion strength encamped in unfortified accommodations deep in presumably unfriendly territory.

Still another fact to be considered was that the Chicaza, who could have matched the Spaniards man for man on the basis of a simple head count, or even sent more, attacked with three hundred warriors. One of the few inviolate rules of to'li' demands that sides be equal in number and ability. As further evidence in that regard, the records admit the Oshpaani' had noticed our warriors keeping close account of them over the preceding weeks, sometimes watching from afar, sometimes making visits under various pretenses, always certainly gathering intelligence. The size of the Chicaza force, then, could fairly be appreciated as a result of careful reconnoitering and calculation, and emphatic proof of a standard of fairness, even if the concern for it was likely unilateral.

In any case, the character of the battle, and the rematch after still another lengthy intermission to allow de Soto and his men to recuperate, resonates with the relationship between to'li' and war as Chickasaws practice them. It was much closer and far more significant than Europeans could discern through cultural lenses that refracted their observations into a familiar, predetermined spectrum.

Even if the breeding, conditioning, and training of Chickasaw warriors might have seemed familiar—Europeans instantly declared a match for them with the militaristic rigors of the Spartans of ancient Greece—they remained a puzzle to the Western mind. Chickasaws did not make war the same way the Europeans did. In fact, they often made a point of refusing to.

Europeans hardly could understand that Chickasaw warriors established a rarefied and shared reputation within the Southeastern culture not only by success against strong, robust enemies like the Oshpaani', but also upon adamant confidence, underpinned by a tribal culture that had served us well, past memory. Even in decisive victory we left to our opponents a reserve of strength, by custom. Such was also the case in stickball, wherein games ended with the sides more or less intact and certainly at equal strength, and parting with the fearless expectation there would be a next time, every time. Our customs baffled Europeans, whose goal or strategy of annihilation, particularly against a worthy enemy, seemed alien to us. To Chickasaws, strategies of annihilation smacked of distasteful, overbearing martial ambition, especially if applied to every conflict, and worse, a disappointing characteristic of poorer cultures that lacked the confidence, and therefore the moral strength, to survive with honor and propriety. To destroy a strong enemy was to destroy one's own strength. The esteem accorded to the Chickasaw, and other great nations around them, was customarily reckoned upon, and confirmed by, the reputations and strengths of our present opponents.

The Chicaza seemed sorry to see de Soto and his team depart to the west, the direction that people of the Southeast traditionally regard as toward loss and death. Perhaps to entice them into returning for a third battle, we took the Spaniards' collective name—Oshpaani'—and gave it to the warrior clan. We have your name; we invite you to return and try to win it back. The Spaniards quit the field. Soon after, de Soto fulfilled the Chicaza's suspicion concerning his direction of departure. He died, and his body was lowered into the Mississippi River, whose waters would yet fail to carry him out of reach of our tribe's dominance. Chickasaws would hold effective control over his burial spot for more than another two hundred years. The conquistador lay ultimately conquered, and the Chickasaw warrior clan kept the name Oshpaani' like a trophy, won fair and square.

The point is that unlike European sports, which are generally considered as playing a certainly ancillary, if sometimes helpfully illustrative, role in culture, to'li' was not, is not, and will never be an extracurricular activity for Chickasaws. It is an essential part of life and an indispensable key to understanding our perspective. To'li' remains, even persists, as something much closer to the peoples' bones

By William A. Crafts, *Burial of De Soto*, Published by Samuel Walker and Company.

than a pastime, rooted so deeply in the ages we share no technical recollection of its origin. We have the intuitive and instructive stories that help us to understand life, our culture, and our world, and some talk about the game. However, a definitive account of its origin, particularly one that supplies technical details, either is missing or concealed among private stories preserved within families or among privileged audiences.

After all, Chickasaws tend to care far more about just getting out on the field and playing the game. After James Adair, the trader with a pen in his hand and a book on his mind, came to live among our ancestors in the Homeland about two centuries after the Spaniards were sent packing, he saw enough to'li' to declare it as "their chief and most favorite game … [and] such severe exercise, as to shew it was originally calculated for a hardy and expert race of people, like themselves." Adair clearly preferred it to another popular Chickasaw game, chunkey. A pastime that demands strength, skill, and keen anticipation, chunkey amounts to a helpful exercise for hunters or warriors. However, to Adair, it suffered in comparison with to'li'. He dismissed chunkey as a "stupid drudgery." As it is said, there is no accounting for taste.

Regardless, Chickasaws would continue to play chunkey and especially to'li', whether in competition between clans or with other villages or against representative groups from other tribes, with untroubled regularity, until a fateful game about sixty years after the accomplishment of officially forced removal from the Homeland to territory in what would become south central Oklahoma.

Up to 1903, four years before the statehood of Oklahoma became an instituted formality, Chickasaws and our more numerous neighbors the Choctaws had settled into a custom of playing traditional, "east-west" games each fall and spring. That brand of game is considered as closest to

George Catlin, during a visit among the Choctaw circa 1834, sketched the basis for three depictions of a ball play, this being the first. The painting presents a tableau of ceremonies before play begins. It shows the equal strengths of the teams and supporters, the elders or leaders forming a sort of barrier between them, and a collection of items set down for wager on the game.

By George Catlin, *Ball-Play Dance*, Renwick Gallery, Washington, D.C.

Photo courtesy of Chickasaw Nation archives.

the prototype of to'li', with its list of solemn injunctions and rituals. As Adair and later writers like Horatio Bardwell Cushman noted, the games would easily career into rough-edged violence, although on the whole, everyone involved did notably well at keeping retributive impulses in harness with good humor and equanimity. Wagering, which is best appreciated as a simple demonstration of Native fan support, was a reliable constant. The invaders considered it problematic and—for all the far riskier gambling Europeans were infamous for—dared to characterize it as shocking. Cushman clucked, "The Chickasaws were addicted to one vice, the vice of gambling. They bet on the proper handling and the skillful shuffling of [a player's] ball-sticks, the fleetness of his feet, and his power of endurance."

The consigning of such a routine demonstration of identification to the province of vice reveals, in stark terms, the differences between Chickasaw and colonial cultures. To Chickasaws, the matter was simple. The wager of everything one owned was, by its character, a mere reflection of the commitment paid in principle, and often in actual terms, by the players and warriors. It was an implicit symbol of a common cultural perspective. It was nice for the supporters to win at their wagers, and dispiriting and perhaps even temporarily calamitous to lose, but either way they did so in parallel company with their players and warriors. Here again Chickasaws proved that the strength of our culture relied in great part on the unbreakable fibers of connection between the peoples of the villages, clans, or tribes and the players or warriors whom, Adair noted significantly, were named and regarded as "beloved." Chickasaws played, risked, won, and lost in community strength.

The sanctimonious disapproval by the colonials also offers an important clue to understanding the results and consequences of the game between the Chickasaws and Choctaws in the spring of 1903 on a plot of land now

George Catlin made at least a few portraits of the standout Choctaw tollih player "Drinks Water From the Stone," of which this is one. In this he wears a turban common among Southeastern Natives of the day.

known as Kullihoma, six miles northwest of the small town of Allen, Oklahoma.

Cushman had written about a similar mass fight that broke out during a game between Choctaws and Creeks more than a century earlier. The leaders of the tribes at the time allowed all who so desired to keep duking it out, releasing them to squander their energies until the following morning, when all were enjoined to quit and go home. By the game in 1903, it seems, pre-emptive measures had come into place, impelled by the settlers' predisposition toward preclusion of any disturbance, thus invoking a talisman of security that would only grow stronger. Lighthorse officers, the official police of the Five Tribes, stood by on alert, as did federal marshals. According to Orel Busby, a jurist and writer who said he interviewed two men who claimed to have been present at the game in 1903, a Chickasaw player at some point struck a Choctaw opponent with his sticks, committing a foul that led to the subsequent disorder, and the lighthorse and marshals were called forth.

More than a hundred years later, details of the incident and its aftermath are only discussed in cursory, tight-lipped summary, and little evidence exists to suggest things were ever otherwise. The east-west games at Kullihoma between the neighboring tribes came to a flat stop, presumably under official pressure from the predominant settler culture. The marshals could not have been happy to deal with such a large and messy disturbance. It also is reasonable to believe that other officials, particularly those with greater authority, began to grumble in favor of regulating the tribes' gatherings, even to the point of prohibiting certain kinds. That last idea presented a popular and attractive option to settlers, even and especially the ones who considered themselves to be magnanimous toward Natives. Their logic tended to characterize such restriction as an impetus toward Native progress, which in brief meant the forced march of Chicka-

A picture of a Choctaw team of traditional stickball players, circa 1903. It cannot be said for certain whether this team was involved in the 1903 game near Kullihoma that closed the tradition of such contests between Choctaws and Chickasaws for a century. However, a Choctaw player who testified he took part in that game, named Mose Burris, is identified as the second man standing on the left in this photo.

Photo courtesy of Chickasaw Nation archives.

A photo of a game, presumably including Chickasaws, said to be played on a baseball field in Emet, Oklahoma, circa the 1940s at the earliest. The placement of the goal post seen here, well down the third-base line toward home plate, indicates this was a two-goal game. Note some are playing in their socks, with trousers tucked into the cuffs. One partially obscured player on the right wears a broad-brimmed hat; others wear scarves tied about their heads, many with single feathers attached. The shorts, which appear to be cutoffs pulled on over their pants (or even union suits) may stand for breechcloths, and may have been the manner in which teams were identified.

Photo courtesy of Chickasaw Nation archives.

saws and Choctaws into eventual lockstep with the invaders' prevailing notions of civilization and, according to the script, achievement of what Europeans termed "equality." Chickasaws, for our part, hardly needed to be reminded of the histories of such matters from our perspective. The debris of similar ideas and intentions lay strewn along a trail from our newer, non-Native land, across the great Mississippi River, back in distance and time to our Homeland that, before we were compelled by scribblings on paper to leave it, already laid diminished by bits and bites, because we believed the promises that other men of putative authority kept making to us.

Worse, the game faced other existential threats. As historian Michael Lovegrove wrote in his award-winning *A Nation in Transition: Douglas Henry Johnston and the Chickasaws, 1898-1939*, the year 1903 also was fraught with political diversions and controversies within the Chickasaw Nation, and some quite troubling. The matter of authentic tribal membership was just one of the evils and controversies arising from the Pandora's box pried open by the process of land allotment enforced by the federal commission named for Henry Dawes, a senator from Massachusetts deeply interested in the so-called "Indian problem." The work and presence of the Dawes Commission energized an undercurrent of the looming eventuality of Oklahoma statehood and its concomitant, grimly practical vow to at last erase Chickasaws as a tribe and nation. Even the more traditionally minded tribal citizens could see what was about to happen. So perhaps with a gathering, two-hearted storm of culture and governance in view, Chickasaws withdrew to'li' into the more secretive folds of our culture, to follow the private stories and the counsels of applications of forest medicines that preceded it. As Ric Greenwood, a coach and leader of the Chickasaw Nation's present revival of Chikasha to'li' said, the game "went to sleep." There it

A monument commissioned and placed by the Chickasaw Nation and the Chickasaw Historical Society marks the general location of the game in 1903 that ended several years of Choctaw-Chickasaw contests of traditional to'li'.

Photo courtesy of Chickasaw Nation archives.

lay, for the implicit purpose of keeping it beyond the grasping, indiscriminately destructive reach of an invasive colonial culture that had failed to understand it ever since de Soto.

The sleep of to'li' proved restless. Adam Walker, a Chickasaw who entered the Chickasaw Nation Hall of Fame in 1997 on the strength of his work as an artist and preserver of the tribe's culture, is recorded as one who kept its traditions not only by crafting the kapochcha'—the curious sticks that are the game's most recognizable symbol—and some items of player regalia, but also by staging several social-style games near his home close to Kullihoma. As Joshua Hinson, present director of the Chickasaw Nation's efforts for language revitalization, and a dedicated player of the traditional game, wrote in his seminal thesis about to'li':

> From the turn of the twentieth century to just prior to the Second World War, the lapse of the matched east-west games and loss of initiated Chickasaw doctors capable of performing the ceremonies and doctoring necessary for ceremonial ground life, including ball play, were significant factors in the changing face of Chickasaw ceremonialism. … The grounds at Kullihoma and Two Ponds were "put to sleep" as was the intertribal ground at Yellow Hill, but in the northern part of the Chickasaw Nation the conservatism of the Kullihoma families helped ensure the viability of Chickasaw ball game and night dance cycles into the present…
>
> According to [Adam] Walker, stickball was played regularly at his home into the late 1980s.

Before his death in 1999, Walker told Glenda Galvan, the Nation's premier storyteller, how those games included and repeated many community-centered traditions of our

A photo of a team probably taken about 1900. Note the breechcloths and the pendant tails or tufts, perhaps horsetail. The sticks are of Choctaw-Chickasaw make, but the studio mark on the photo frame indicates the team is likely Choctaw. Note the man on the far right wears a gun belt with bullets inserted in the loops, possibly indicating his status as a lighthorse officer.

Photo courtesy of Chickasaw Nation archives.

tribe's past. As spirited as they might have been, they were informal, single-pole social events and often allowed women to play, although they would not use the sticks. Still, as Hinson's thesis noted, Walker's games provided an important practical method for preserving at least the memory of the skills necessary to play the game.

After the twenty-first century began, precisely a hundred years after the last traditional game before to'li' "went to sleep" in Chickasaw culture, the Nation's historical society sponsored and organized a "demonstration game" between a team of tribal members—including Hinson, among other leaders and future captains of the Nation's cultural renaissance—and a team of Choctaw players, at Kullihoma during the annual event called Chikasha Ittafama, the Chickasaw Reunion. The game, played under a soaking mid-June rain, looked far different from the ones of 1903 and earlier, yet it and other, similar games for several following years would establish prescient cultural milestones.

The present resurgence of stickball among Chickasaws found strength and speed in 2008, about five years after the rainy game at Kullihoma, especially among communities within the Nation's boundaries in south central Oklahoma. Chickasaws demonstrated enthusiasm for a rediscovered touchstone of their culture by traveling, often quite far, to meet athletes and teams from other tribes who played the two-stick game. Soon many who would become leaders of the grass-roots renaissance of to'li', including Jeremy Wallace, Ric Greenwood, Brad Greenwood, and Brandon White Eagle, began to host social games and practices at Kullihoma and other fields in and near the Nation's headquarters city of Ada.

The zeal and dedication of the players, and of the executives and departments of the Nation who worked to support them, met more difficult realities of logistics like provision for equipment, travel, and other practical concerns common among team sports, especially in the process of growing. In early 2013, Lisa John, then newly appointed as secretary of culture and humanities, and Lori Hamilton, also just named executive officer of the division of history and culture, met to discuss and develop a plan to support Chikasha to'li', much in same way the Nation's cultural resources department had supported stomp dancing as a custom and a cultural exhibition, for almost two decades by then.

After all, John reasoned, stomp dancing, itself a deeply significant and spiritual custom of the Chickasaw, was part of the rich cultural atmosphere of stickball, especially during great games of the past that were accompanied by all-night dancing and singing. She and Hamilton sought to bring balance to the division's support of the equally crucial cultural traditions, and with that in mind, John brought the matter to the attention of Governor Bill Anoatubby, and proposed to him that the Nation should sponsor an official stickball team, as it did for the stomp dance troupe. Moreover, she and Hamilton presented to the governor a plan to teach Chickasaw youth not only to play the game, but also to learn its cultural significance among our people and other Southeastern nations.

Governor Anoatubby acted at once to support the team and the game's opportunities for Chickasaw youth and adults, and by the summer of 2013 Chikasha Toli became an official program within the cultural resources department of the history and culture division, on a level with the Nation's exemplary stomp dance troupe and exhibitions. In the next year, the division of history and culture officially launched Chikasha Bak Bak, the youth stickball team named for the legendary woodpecker of the Southeast, long considered a friend and guardian of the Chickasaw. The division's executives and managers soon worked to satisfy swiftly mounting demands for instructional meetings about stickball, often in the larger communities found within the Chickasaw Nation,

A photo of a game said to have been played in Emet, Oklahoma, in 1940. Note the pole at the left, the height of which indicates this is a two-goal game. Also, note no women are present. The arrangement and action of players indicates the photo may have been taken at the moment the ball was thrown upward to begin play.

Photo courtesy of Chickasaw Nation archives.

like Sulphur, Tishomingo, Newcastle, and Ada. White Eagle, Ric Greenwood, and Clovis Hamilton, all instructors in Hinson's language program, accepted responsibilities as players and coaches of the adult and youth teams and as leaders of other on-field programs, including revival of the traditional east-west game.

Though veterans at teaching Chikashshanompa', the language of the Chickasaw, Greenwood and Clovis Hamilton admitted their experiences with to'li' tended to follow the rise of interest among communities of Chickasaws, and the game at once became a matter of research for them.

"I didn't grow up playing stickball at all," Hamilton said one fall afternoon after the close of the season for Chikasha Bak Bak, for which he served as the principal coach. "I didn't know anything about it, growing up. I didn't start playing it until, like, around 2010 or so."

Greenwood acknowledged the same concerning himself and noted how the new interest in to'li' developed with surprising speed, as if impelled by the game's own inscrutable energy of emergence from its fitful, century-long sleep. In the meantime, Chikasha Toli and Chikasha Bak Bak have grown, although hardly at unmanageable rates. Its return to popularity and practice, however steady, has brought to'li' into full confrontation with a set of cultural obstacles that had only begun to arise a hundred years ago. Distractions offered by the surrounding predominant culture, from technological diversions to hordes of other organized sports, have to this point regulated Chikasha Bak Bak's numbers, as Clovis Hamilton noted. "It's hard enough," he said, "to get thirty boys to come out to play," referring to a preferable number for a roster that also includes girls of school age.

According to Lori Hamilton, players on the Chikasha Toli team began in about 2013 to stress an interest in representing Chickasaws on a tribal level, much like Choctaw Nation teams in Oklahoma and Mississippi do, particular-

Youth stickball teams include female and male players. Here, during a game between Chikasha Bak Bak and a youth team of the Choctaw Nation, a Bak Bak defender pursues a player of the Choctaw team headed downfield with the ball held in the sticks. Note the players are wearing socks, adhering to the rule against cleats or other footwear that might injure others, especially in close situations called "scrums."

Photo by Branden Hart

Photo by Branden Hart

ly at grand competitions like the World Series of Stickball. The tournament is held each year in Choctaw, Mississippi, about fifty miles south of the southernmost boundary of the ancient Chickasaw Homeland in that state. As a result, Chikasha Toli, as the Nation's official team, began to be structured like Choctaw teams which, significantly, also allow women to play the two-stick game.

Although Chikasha Toli is well into play against similar teams from other Southeastern tribes, it has yet to appear in competitions like the Mississippi tournament. In the meantime, Ric Greenwood and his brother Brad—known to friends as "Ace"—and a handful of others have represented Chikasha Toli at the Series by taking part as players on some Choctaw teams.

The quickness at which all of it seemed to occur hardly affected the focus on another ultimate and rather daunting goal, which was to revive the game in its most solemn manner and sense—the full realization of the traditional east-west game, with its attendant customs and ceremony.

Clovis Hamilton, White Eagle, the Greenwoods, and their fellow players in Chikasha Toli at once appreciated the vastness of that undertaking. They faced immediate problems encountered among other, similar quests within Native tribes to restore, if perhaps not always to precisely recreate, cultural interests and pursuits of the past. One of the first and hardest problems would be to gain knowledge of initiations and ceremonies that the alikchi' and hopayi'— our medical and spiritual professionals, at the time—kept so closely bound within their exclusive fraternity that many have been lost to time and the peremptory erasures imposed by manifest destiny and the benign neglect of incuriosity prominent within the culture of colonization.

"We're doing this based on our research and knowledge," Ric Greenwood said. "And we're modifying it, because there are certain things we can't do, and we'll never

A Chikasha Bak Bak player prepares to execute a proper throw downfield with the kapochcha'. Note the placement of the sticks and the hands.

be able to do, because those practices are gone. We hope that as we progress and continue to have these games, that we learn something new and add to it.

"I did some research," he added. "I found a few videos and talked to some Creeks and Seminoles that I know, because they still play their traditional game, with their four dances. Josh [Hinson] said we follow a lot of their practices, so to speak."

Among those practices are some that could hardly be concealed from non-Native observers like Adair or Cushman. As an example, for a prescribed number of days before each ball play—as before every mission undertaken by our warriors—the players would submit to a systematic regime of fasting, abstinence, separation, and purification. Layers of significance present themselves in this tradition of the game, one of its clearest demonstrations of blood kinship with the ceremonies of war.

The warriors of the Chickasaw Homeland were also usually at least as dedicated to playing to'li'. As proud and exclusive as their brotherhood certainly was, their custom of preparation for battle or ball play was crafted by time and culture and meant to elevate their status within their tribe and also their personal spiritualities. Fasting rendered warriors' bodies lighter and lifted their souls free of the bonds of earthly sustenance. Abstinence trained the warrior's spirit to work alone. Separation has always been the meaning of holiness, the dedication to significant principles. Purging rid their bodies and spirits of sundry incidental poisons and contaminations, laying aside the weights that so easily beset them. All such deprivations and denials they suffered, accepting them with tempered enthusiasm, in the name of a fundamental cultural understanding that only the pure are fit for sacrifice, whether on the battlefield or the ball field. All of it was done for the sake of the people in whose behalf they played or fought.

Teams of adult players pass each other, touching sticks, after a game between Chikasha Toli and the Tvshka Homma team from the Choctaw Nation.

Photo by Branden Hart

The Chikasha Bak Bak team during the spring of 2016. Members range in age from seven to seventeen years, although some teenage players also may play for the adult Chikasha Toli team, if approved.

Photo by Branden Hart

Those customs seemed to present an extreme and often impenetrable example to the Europeans, who in a short time would gain the upper cultural hand by strength of numbers. Generations of exposure to the invaders' culture—which, despite its reflexive statements of respect for the principle of self-denial, rarely recommends its practice to such degrees as ours—have rendered many modern Chickasaws either unwilling or, in cases traceable to health reasons, unable to imitate what our warriors did. Hamilton and Greenwood discovered as much while they and several other men prepared for the first of what they seek to establish as a series of traditional east-west games.

They staged the game during the traditional time of Chikasha Ittafama, the Chickasaw Reunion, in mid-spring of 2015 at Kullihoma. By agreement, the players amended the requirements of preparation to a day of fasting before the game, and half that for anyone who could not fast as long without risks to health. Purging, which squeamish Europeans wrote was achieved by drinking draught after draught of a tea said to be brewed from the leaves of a plant bearing the unappetizing scientific name *ilex vomitoria*, was set aside, at least for the time.

About six months later, Greenwood went down a list of matters that could see changes and adjustments before they would stage the next traditional game. "The goal," he explained, "is to experience what it was like in a traditional sense and eventually get to a full, traditional purging, fasting, singing the right songs."

The Chikasha Toli and Chikasha Bak Bak teams he and Hamilton lead play a more structured and modernized version of the game, although still linked firmly to the same origins. Addressing those differences, Greenwood said, "What we're trying to do is show these people that are interested in stickball that what they're seeing now is not traditional. It's just another way to play the game. We want these youths and the people that are playing to know there's another style, another way that we play, if you want to play it, if eventually you want to go through that, experience that."

The leaders of the Chickasaw Nation's growing stickball program have hitherto demonstrated no interest in creating an artificial hierarchy of skill or authenticity. However, the fact remains, as Greenwood would further note, that as the revival of the traditional game draws nearer to realization, that game will become more difficult to prepare for, let alone to play.

"If we get it back to the way we'd like to have it," Greenwood told *Chokma*, the Chickasaw Nation's general interest magazine, "as we progress and add more things to it, it makes it harder. So it's really going to challenge you. Do you want to fast for three days? Do you want to purge your body for those three days? Because you're supposed to exclude yourself from anything—you don't put anything in your body other than, really, water."

All methods and measures to be applied toward such a progressive realization of the traditional game were yet to be determined, and everyone involved reasonably expected a continuous, if incremental process of change. The point remained clear that much of the history of Chikasha to'li' had, and has, yet to be written and lived and played. All the developments it might face will arise from an ineluctable energy generated not only by the interest and curiosity of Chickasaws, but also in great part by our success to date, which has been visible.

Although the Chickasaw Nation had fielded organized teams for only a few years, the character and results of the 2015 east-west revival game rewarded the leaders of the stickball renaissance with more encouragement than they may have expected. Only four years earlier, on a nearby field at the same grounds, an invitational stickball tournament generated an internet video full of grimace-inducing tackles among other instances of the kind of rough and amateurish play generally seen among players and clubs of scant experience. That kind of play made almost no appearance on the field at Kullihoma in May 2015. The game, which continued into extended time after a tied score at the end of the set period, presented a consistent emphasis on finesse and awe-inspiring athleticism. Spectators—watching in appreciative quiet, in accordance with their cultural custom—witnessed swift pursuits, skillful handling of the paired sticks, arching long throws, and impossible catches, all marks of veteran teams and players.

"Five years ago, we couldn't catch the ball," Clovis Hamilton recalled six months later. "We'd just try to track it and pick it up off the ground. Now, even if you're like, sixty yards out, you try to catch it and throw it right back. That's just how the skills have evolved over the last few years. And," he added with a smile of satisfaction, "it looks really good when you catch it from that far and throw it back."

The fruits of their progress have lent strength to the further establishment of to'li' as a Chickasaw institution. Early in 2016, during the first conference of the Chickasaw Historical Society, Lisa John, Secretary of the Chickasaw Nation's Department of Culture and Humanities, announced the Nation's plan for what would be its first field dedicated to stickball play and practice. It will be built on newly acquired land adjacent to the Chickasaw Cultural Center in Sulphur, Oklahoma. In addition to the stickball field, the land will be further developed to include areas for traditional games and stomp dance.

"The intent," she said, "is to utilize newly acquired acreage adjacent to the [Chickasaw Cultural Center]. This acreage will also be utilized for camps and other activities, such as educating Chickasaw people and the public about other traditional games the Chickasaws played."

SECTION TWO

UNIFORMS
AND
EQUIPMENT

George Catlin's *Ball-Play of the Choctaw-Ball Up*. Catlin's depiction of a Choctaw game circa 1834 gives at least some insight into what players of the two-stick game looked like in the nineteenth century. The head-dresses seem Plains Indian style, there's more uniformity than he likely saw, and the "tails" worn by the players are likely exaggerated.

By George Catlin, *Ball-Play of the Choctaw-Ball Up*, Smithsonian American Art Museum.

By the time non-Native observers like George Catlin came along about the mid-nineteenth century to record as much as they cared, or dared, about Native culture, most European-based sports had just entered the era of structure and institution their current fans are well familiar with. Contributing to that structure was a general concession to an intuition that spectators might wish to distinguish members of one side of a contest from the other, or at least to understand who belonged on the fields of play. By Catlin's time, about the mid-1830s, cricket players had adopted their "whites," the monochrome business-casual ensemble many wear today. Soccer players still awaited the days of breezy shorts and all but weightless shin pads. About a century would pass before numbers would appear on uniforms, the better to keep track of players, and a little longer than that until names would be helpfully stenciled across the backs of jerseys.

Catlin left to us his keen appreciation for the visual, many examples of which he produced or embellished some weeks or even months after the last of his several trips into the Native interior of his day. He had an eye for artistic record, nonetheless, and seemed drawn not only to the grand spectacle of stickball, but also to the care taken to array some players in uniform, if one accepts a broad definition of the term. The purposes of such dress and array, he assumed, ranged from mere distinction to intimidation, considerations common to his culture's appreciations of the spirit of athletic competition. Interestingly, he also mentioned how the game's goals were marked in such a way that would help players avoid the mistake of scoring goals for their opponents—an infamous hazard, and persistent even among many popular team sports today.

However, as we return to the subject of athletic dress, we realize that to properly consider the kind worn by players of Chikasha to'li', past or present, we must excuse ourselves from the European perspective, and especially its tendency to be fastidious. For example, popular American sports leagues of origins closest to the invaders' traditions might equivocate about matters of personal risk or players' rights, but they routinely insist on stern regulation of work clothes. Jerseys must be tucked, all items of apparel must match—in short, uniforms must look uniform. What the team looks like is considered essential to the collective identity. Culture matters, but not more than, and usually not as much as, brand awareness.

In to'li', however, culture is everything, and branding is regarded from a remote distance. One result of that is the variegated nature of dress one finds on its playing fields. If we consider that to be counter-intuitive, especially for a game intended to reflect and emphasize the culture and tradition of the Chickasaw identity, then we should consider the nature of that identity, and how it relates to the way Chickasaws play the game.

To Chickasaws, teamwork and individuality are not historically opposite or alternative philosophies, but complements. Their warriors went out to fight either alone or in bands, as missions demanded, and every warrior prepared—in fact, expected—to face critical and defining moments that, in many cases, also might result in outright changes of personal identity.

As John Dyson once wrote for *Ishtunowa: The Journal of Chickasaw History and Culture,*

> Boys who were destined to become warriors ... sought to leave their childish names behind, hoping to be known instead by some military deed of theirs that would be both worthy of notice and of subsequent public acclaim. ... [A] child called *Chola* ("Fox") would cease to exist as such when, upon the testimony of eyewitnesses, he was lat-

The way this Mississippi Choctaw player holds his sticks seems intended to give the viewer a good idea of how they are used.

By M.R. Harrington, *Jim Tubby, Mississippi Choctaw*, Smithsonian Institution.

BALL PLAYERS.

By George Catlin, *Ball Players*, Smithsonian American Art Museum, Washington, D.C.

er honored with a name change for a note-worthy feat … let us say by the epithet *Naa-hollabi'* ("He Killed a White Man"). Similarly, *Naahollabi'* would be supplanted when in a later such ritual the warrior was renamed, for example, *Toklo Ishtabi'* ("He Seized Two and Killed Them").

Somewhat like modern professional athletes whose teams, uniforms, and other levels of recognition and reward might change while their accomplishments carry them up or down their sports' peculiar hierarchies, Chickasaw warriors—who usually played stickball, too—pursued a symbiosis of ambition and identification. Thereby they established their legendary reputations, in company and individually, although encountering far less conflict of interest than we suspect of some professionals of our day. The matter had nothing to do with the transactional, and frankly mercenary, relationship we expect in the present realm of athletics and even warfare. The benefits of victory, not to mention the reversals of defeat, were shared. All esteem and regards, including and especially names taken from exploits of bravery, were emblematic of the warriors' places within, and subservient to, their house, their clan, their tribe, and their culture.

Perhaps because of that, combined with reflexive hesitation among the Southeastern people to share everything about their lives and beliefs with invaders whose tendency to be condescending was recognized and noted, the European invaders tended, as if by default, to refer to warriors in collective terms. In hindsight, that may have been a technical cultural mistake.

Whether in battle or to'li', whether tribe against tribe, clan against clan, or village against village, all Chickasaw probably knew what, and more to the point, who to expect. While players approached the field, raising their brave whoops of challenge, elders would point out the famed and

From the Chickasaw collection at the National Museum of the American Indian (Object 02/7627): to'li' imbalaafokha, or ballplayer's pants, described as made of commercial cotton cloth and hand-sewn, perhaps more than a century old. Note the drawstrings at the cuffs and the waist, and especially the raccoon tail affixed to the waistband at the back.

the esteemed to the boys, who in turn were expected by custom to take careful note and to burn with admiration and ambition to be the same, look the same, and perhaps dress the same, one day soon.

"The clothing" they wore, wrote Joshua D. Hinson, in his book, *Chikasha: The Chickasaw Collection at the National Museum of the American Indian*, "are far more than uniforms."

> They are symbols of intent—the intent to engage, dominate, and kill the enemy. In placing them on their bodies, players expressed this intent through red and black— the colors of war—and walked on to the field of play with ball sticks—the weapons of war.

The items at the museum in the book's title include a pair of red shorts notable for drawstring cinches at the waist and legs, and featuring a "pendant raccoon tail" fastened to the middle of the waistband in back. That and another separate tail, of a cougar, reflected a matter of record set down by observers who told us the players often would attach such and similar items (e.g., bird feathers and, sometimes, bat wings) to their clothes and equipment. They thereby followed a custom of supposition that doing so would, as Hinson put it, "gain some aspect of the animal's spiritual power." It also may have helped provide an identifying mark, such as to signify and honor the clan or house to which a player or team belonged, or even perhaps to advertise a player's tactical philosophy. There seemed to be no law against individual imagination or artistic license.

A couple of other pieces discussed in Hinson's book provide examples of a certain item of regalia one was guaranteed to find at a Chickasaw ball play, even many decades after removal from the Homeland. They are examples of the breechcloth, which some non-Native observers called

"breechclouts," and Chickasaws who actually wore them called tikba-takaali', along with the belts, or askoffa, that held them up, and of course were at least as important. The specimens at the NMAI are especially crafted for use by stickball players, and thus earn the name to'li' intikba-takaa-li' askoffa ta'wwa'w, which translates roughly into English as "ball-player's breechcloth with belt." Each tikba-takaali' looks like James Adair's description, "a slip of cloth, about a quarter of an ell wide, and an ell and an half long," the archaic "ell" being a measure of about forty-five inches. The cloths at the NMAI are slightly tapered toward each end, and the edges of each are trimmed with strips of contrasting color—either black or dark blue—about an inch wide. Similar darker strips are also stitched into "T"-shape motifs at their ends.

To'li' intikba-takaali' of similar color, design, and motif were worn by players at the Chickasaw Nation's revival of the traditional east-west game at Kullihoma in May 2015. The teams were distinguished by them, one side wearing red (homma') breechcloths with black (losa') trim and the other reversing the scheme, their tikba-takaali' made of black cloth with red trim and motifs.

The players also wore representations of another item of Chickasaw stickball regalia found at the museum: the to'li' iminno'chi', a separate collar to which was attached long shreds of red cloth, set in a radiating pattern to lay about the player's shoulders, upper back, and clavicle. Among the Seminoles, Hinson was told, such a collar was worn with an intent to absorb and disguise any flow of blood on or about that part of the body, which at least some must have appreciated as a customary hazard of the traditional game.

Chickasaws wore them, too, as the artifact at NMAI indicates, although Hinson took care to note, cannily, that no one has so far confirmed whether they did so for the same reasons. He believed the red cloth collar was devel-

Also from the Chickasaw collection at NMAI (Object 03/2645), this to'li' imin-no'chi'—a collar of shredded cotton cloth, from about the same period as the pants on page 44—was worn loosely tied around a player's neck, and was easily detachable.

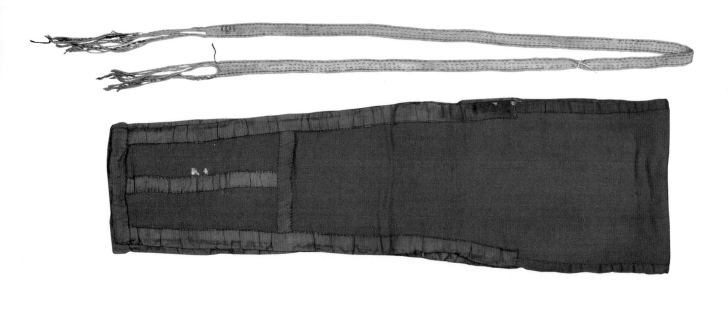
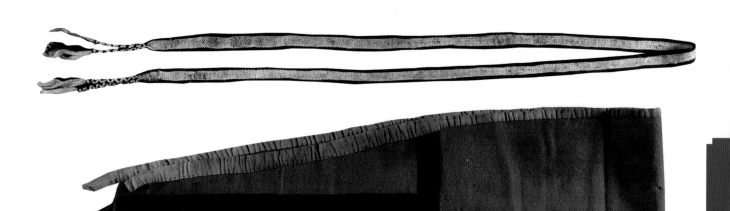

oped during a more or less modern time—say, a little before the turn of the twentieth century—as a replacement for, or perhaps a symbol of, a similar piece fashioned from porcupine quills or strands from a horse's mane or tail and worn by players of the game's deeper past. The idea of using the porcupine's trademark quills, with their infamous barbs, suggests another, more likely defensive idea behind such a collar. An opposing player might think twice before reaching above or about the shoulders to seize a man wearing one. Besides, the notion of conceding to an idea that a player might need, or even desire, to soak up blood from a superficial injury suffered during play seems odd. Players ignored—and in fact were expected to disregard—minor bleeding, especially from the area concerned. Besides, it could add a tactical benefit. A player coated with blood and sweat would be slippery, difficult to grasp or restrain.

Also, the to'li' iminno'chi' and the tikba-takaali' are clearly of a quality that we, these days, call "tearaway" athletic gear, which modern institutions of sports have tended to regard as a recent innovation. Yet, behold: the earliest known dispensable athletic apparel—on this continent, anyway. The collars and breechcloths, for whatever purposes they fulfilled at other times, became optional once the ball was served up to begin play. As durable as they might have been, they were engineered to come off easily in an opponent's grip, without interrupting the erstwhile wearer's momentum or movement, leaving him free to play as naked as a Greek of the ancient Olympic games.

A similar option for athletic wear seemed common for the players' feet. Catlin's depictions of the players and the game appear to indicate that at least most players took the field in bare feet. He introduces some confusion, although we already understand he often embellished for the benefit of what he thought his audiences wanted to see, by showing players wearing some sort of foot or ankle adornments in

At left, two examples of to'li' intikba-takaali' askoffa ta'wwa'w (upper NMAI Object 03/2628; lower NMAI Object 03/2629), or ballplayers' breechcloths with belts, also perhaps more than a century in age. Note the borders and "T"-shape motifs and the slender belts. These also were worn with a mind toward being easily detachable.

one of the three paintings he produced to record a grand-scale Choctaw game in the mid-1830s. In the other two, the players wear no moccasins or anklets. His portrait of a prominent Choctaw player involved in that game indicates the man played barefooted. In summary, it seems clear that the players decided individually whether to play with foot gear and if so, it either was an anklet or pair of moccasins. It might also be fair to consider that, as durable as moccasins can be, they do take time and diligence to craft, and a player might have hesitated to subject his pair to the rigors and accidents of rough ball play.

The footwear option has survived, and indeed kept its prevalence, among the tribes who play the two-stick game. Its persistence has led to a more or less codified rule, to insist that shoes with ground-grabbing cleats of any kind may not be worn on the field. The matter concerns more than the supposed advantages that cleats might give a player. A look at a scrum of players in pursuit of a grounded ball demonstrates the point of the rule. In such a close situation, people's feet get stepped on, repeatedly, and any athlete who has suffered the bite of a cleated shoe can describe the resulting pain.

The bare foot also was an everyday matter for most Chickasaws for much of the year, especially in the Deep-South Homeland. The same went for the clothing and items they wore during games. All of them reflected the warriors' and players' recognition of and response toward an expectation of the people they protected and played for—to be prepared to go into action, at any time. What a warrior wore each day were the essentials for his battle or game uniform, awaiting only the solemnities of preparation. As Hinson noted in his 2007 thesis about Chickasaw stickball equipment and regalia, the described

> regalia ensemble is virtually identical to the
> war regalia of an eighteenth-century *tash-*

Naki Greenwood breaks upfield with the ball held in his sticks during a ball play on the grounds of the Chickasaw National Capitol Building in Tishomingo, Oklahoma. Teammate Dale Shackleford follows behind him.

Photo by Joshua Clough

ka Chikashsha (Chickasaw warrior), regalia comprised of a [*tikba*]-*takaali'* and *yaatala* [i.e., feathers worn on the head or in a hat]. War regalia were simply items of everyday clothing modified through the act of ceremonial war preparation … The ceremonial war function of *to'li' Chikashsha ịnaafokha* [i.e., Chickasaw stickball regalia] continues to the present and includes everyday cotton t-shirts and shorts modified to become ball play clothes.

In that paragraph Hinson distills two major premises of his seminal work. One establishes the kinship between war (tanap) and to'li' as so close it blurs every boundary of distinction, and the other emphasizes that the most enduring character of the Chickasaw cultural context "negates the classification of Chickasaw art as 'traditional' or 'non-traditional'; instead, these things that we have made and continue to make are simply 'Chikashsha,'" as he says elsewhere in his thesis.

Of Chikashsha things made then and now, none demonstrate those principles better than the kapochcha'—the players' sticks that give us the most popular and well-recognized emblem of to'li'. They begin as slender lengths of hickory (osak) harvested during the cold months while sap is down, and cut to lengths between four and five feet and about an inch square. The wood of the pecan, which Chickasaws called osak falaa, thus identifying it as a variety of hickory, or the bois d'arc (itti' lakna') also will do.

The process and results of stick-making teach a great deal about distinctions between the crafts of the Five Tribes, all of which play the two-stick game. Cherokees, for example, produce sticks that examination reveals to be quite different from ones made by the other four. Hinson wrote that Cherokee ball play sticks are:

A pair of kapochcha', from the Chickasaw collection at the NMAI (Object 02/7503), are of Chickasaw-Choctaw manufacture. Note the placement of the "shoulder"—the piece below the cup that joins to the handle—that marks this set of sticks as probably made for a right-handed player. Also note how one stick is about an inch shorter than the other.

A detail from an illustration curated by the Holisso Center for the Study of Chickasaw History and Culture in Sulphur, Oklahoma, shows three different styles of sticks as used by the five Southeastern tribes for their two-stick game. On the left are characteristic Cherokee-style sticks with their hairpin-like construction and intricate webbing; on the right are the Creek-Seminole fashion, with their long "shoulders." In the center are Chickasaw-Choctaw sticks with their shorter shoulders, simpler webbing and slender cups.

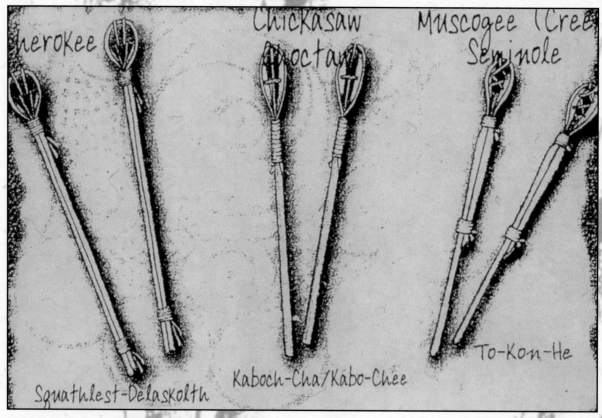

Photo courtesy of Chickasaw Nation archives.

traditionally made using a hickory wood blank measuring at least five to six feet in length. The cups are formed at the center of this blank, which when thinly carved and bent to shape, forms the two-part handle. The handles are worked until an essentially seamless mating of the two opposing inner surfaces is achieved. The two handle sections are then generally secured with nails or wooden pegs. The standard lacing pattern involves two vertical passes of leather or occasionally wire … which are then crossed with one or two horizontal passes to create the net. Cherokee sticks are generally made the same length.

Seminoles and Creeks build sticks that come somewhat closer to the Chickasaws' and Choctaws' fashion. They are, Hinson wrote,

made using a hickory wood blank measuring approximately five feet in length. The cups are formed [beginning] approximately six inches back from the end of the blank. A small extension is generally left intact at the end of the blank to ensure the leather binding does not slip. The wood left intact at the bottom left and right of the cup forms the characteristic "shoulder" of the Muscogee (Creek) – Seminole ball stick.

The cups of Creek and Seminole sticks are usually crafted to appear more slender and perhaps a little deeper than those of the Cherokees, with a more pronounced flare—the angle of their sides away from the center at the back of the stick, where the ball would rest—and the tilt of the cups toward the inner faces of their handles seems a bit more pronounced. The combination may give the catching and throwing end of the stick somewhat the same quality as the much larger basket-woven *cesta* wielded by players of the swift Basque game of *jai alai*, lending the ball a reliable path for reception or delivery. That aspect is seen also in Choctaw- and Chickasaw-made sticks, although the resemblance ends at that point. Like the Cherokees, the Creeks and Seminoles by custom fashion their handles to be round, and their lacing—the webbing inside the cups—has taken on a more intricate, diamond-pattern motif, especially among sticks made in the present day.

In comparison, then, Choctaw and Chickasaw sticks, which from one to the other seem all but indistinguishable in manufacture and appearance, appear simpler. Their blanks are left square, although they usually are sanded for the sake of comfort in the grip and are often tapered from the handle to the cup. The tapering, aesthetically pleasing as it might appear, is a practical feature, rendering the handles less likely to slip out of a player's grip involuntarily. Their cups are formed somewhat like the Creeks' and Seminoles', although with a shorter shoulder lashed to the handle to form the throat. The lacing inside the cup is most usually a simple, single cross of leather strip, wire, sturdy twine, or whatever kind of cord the maker or player prefers.

From generalities we proceed to the details of ka-pochcha', and details matter. For example, the shoulders, those parts of the original blanks to be lashed to the handles below their cups, should appear on the left when the sticks are held in the hands of a right-handed player with the faces of their cups looking upward. (For a left-handed player, they should be on the right, although Clovis Hamilton—the coach of the youth Chikasha Bak Bak team, and a player and stick-maker—said many left-handers, like himself, have learned to play with right-handed sticks.) The reason is technical. Right-handers tend to catch with the left and throw from the right. Because touching the to'wa' (ball) with ei-

This photo is identified by title as "Mississippi Choctaw ball player." Note the cap with single feather, the abbreviated breechcloth, and pants with cuffs gathered over bare feet. His sticks are of classic Choctaw-Chickasaw make and right-handed. Note also that one is visibly shorter than the other.

Photo courtesy of Chickasaw Nation archives.

ther hand, and certainly both, is unforgivably proscribed, to catch and secure the ball often involves bringing both sticks together at the cups, coordinating the hands, the eyes, and the fruits of practice with one's equipment into an action somewhat like an alligator's jaws snapping a leaping fish out of midair. Because a right-handed player is likely to bring the cup of the right stick down upon the left in that instance to secure the to'wa', a proper construction places the shoulders on the outside of either stick, away from incident of impact, and thus avoiding obstruction and wear and tear.

For that reason, and a common likelihood that the player might need to throw the to'wa' quickly after catching it, the stick held in the throwing hand is often made a little shorter than its mate, if only by perhaps an inch. In throwing, the ball often is kept between the cups of both sticks while they are lifted, held together in a rotation that at its apex finds them slung over the player's throwing shoulder. Thus the throwing hand comes nearest the shoulder, and a shorter stick helps ensure the cups stay together for as long as needed.

The cups, besides being the most distinctive features of kapochcha', bring the craft of stick-making to a focus. The blanks, the raw forms from which the sticks are made, must be without blemishes, especially knots, or any unevenness in quality. They cannot be of heartwood—from the center of the tree's trunk—because it lacks porousness and is not as flexible as the craft demands, most particularly when it comes to fashioning the cups. Hinson took detailed measurements of the sticks catalogued at the NMAI for *Chikasha*, and thereby revealed graceful tapering from the handle to the cup, wherein he recorded an almost delicate thickness of about an eighth of an inch. The shoulder ends were marked by notches set apart to secure the leather-strip lashing at the throat. Another, higher notch helped to secure the bottom end of the longitudinal course of the

A detail is taken and enhanced from a rough sketch concerning stickball manufacture curated by the Holisso Center. In it, we find details about where the materials for the blanks are taken, either from hickory or bois d'arc trees. Note the drawings indicate that the heartwood—the core of the trunk—should be avoided.

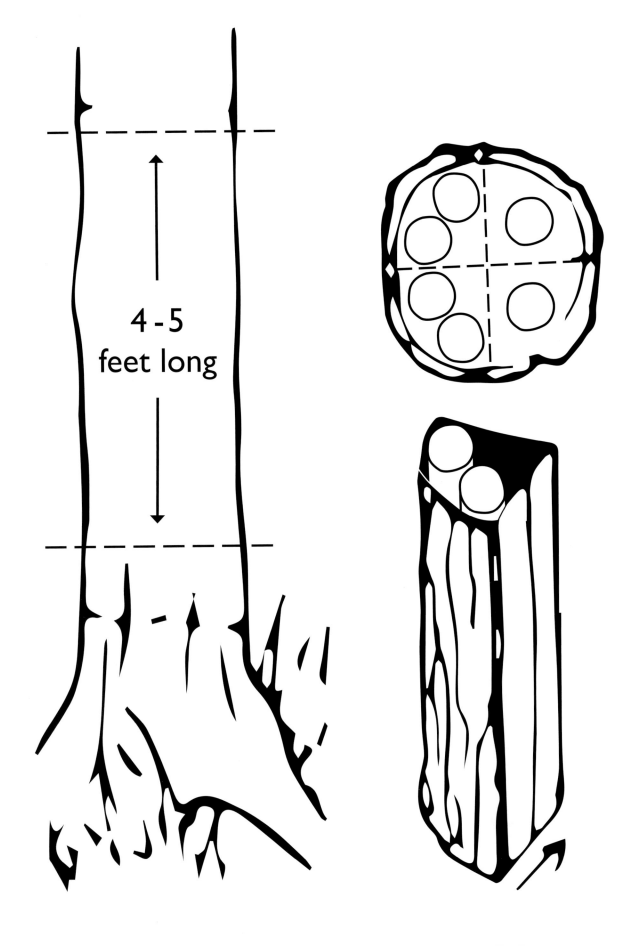

4 - 5
feet long

Photo by Wakeah Vigil

webbing inside the cup. The crafting of wood in that manner seems similar to the care and work necessary to make a bow (tanampa̲lhlhi'), although Chickasaws tended to favor the less pliant heartwood for that because it lent greater draw strength and, as Hinson noted, bowmakers also paid careful attention to the alignment of growth rings. It is easy to conjecture that a Chickasaw skilled in crafting tanampa̲lhlhi' might also be sought out to produce kapochcha'.

Even the most diligent description of the details of kapochcha' or their craft could not make clear the conspiracy of time, work, care, and education necessary to the manufacture of a single set. Clovis Hamilton ruefully admitted to frustrations he suffered during his initiation as a kapochcha' maker. For one of his introductory experiences, his long hours of dedicated work to prepare a stick up to the most critical point in the process—the bending of the wood to form the cup—ended in deflating discouragement when it snapped like a toothpick. "That was a long time to put in," he recalled, his tone still simmering with chagrin. "Eight hours of work, and I got nothing out of it but firewood. Right then and there, I wanted to quit—forever. But I stayed with it, and I'm getting better. I'm still not good enough that I can turn out consistently good pairs."

Hamilton's impressive production of self-crafted kapochcha', including two exquisite pairs (one for a right-handed player; the other left-handed) he submitted for the Chickasaw Nation's Te Ata Fisher Employee Art Show and competition in 2016, indicated he applied much humility to his discussion about making them. It also established him among the rarest craftsmen in the world. He and fellow player and coach Ric Greenwood, a leader of the team of adult-level players under the name Chickasha Toli, have joined a scant and slowly growing company of makers of sticks dedicated to the Chickasaw game. In their time exist no kits and few shortcuts, and their craft, like many others

A craftsman takes measurements at a workshop where kapochcha' are made. The rough blanks used to make sticks for to'li' are generally cut to about five feet long and an inch square.

A modern band saw is used to begin the process of cutting "blanks" that will be made into kapochcha'. Chickasaws have a history of putting newer technologies to the service of their traditional crafts.

Photo by Wakeah Vigil

in the realm of Chickasaw tribal culture, whether for the sake of ornament or representational art or replication of tools, weapons, or other items of the ancestors' workaday lives, has revealed much about the ancestors' cultural approach toward creativity and utility. Hinson illuminated one principle in his thesis: "to make good sticks one must have good craftsmanship, ilbak chokma," which, translated more or less literally, means "good hand(s)." Even while conveniences of modern tools and technologies are certainly put to use, most authentic ilbak chokma crafts hardly lend themselves to simple or quick manufacture, let alone mass production.

On a bright, chilled January day, a small group of Chickasaws, including Greenwood and Hamilton, took a tidy shipment of several dozen hickory blanks cut to the prescribed lengths and widths and began the lengthy and painstaking process of crafting them into sets of kapoch-cha', a task that, as Hamilton estimated, takes about eight hours of hands-on work, at minimum, for each pair. The assignments for the day would bring the sticks to the actual make-or-break point, carving and bending them to begin making the cups. The spaces on the blanks for their cups were cut, on that day with a band saw, and further carved if necessary to form the thinner section to be bent. Before bending, their tapered ends were steeped in a bath of steaming water to allow the wood to soak enough heat and moisture to avoid breaking.

To begin the cups—loops, more properly—the prepared sticks were brought to a piece of equipment customized to the purpose, a surrogate for the tree limbs of proper size that ancients used. A pipe set in a discarded auto wheel stood to a height of about five and a half feet, with four directly opposing cross pieces welded alternately beginning from about four feet from its base—two small girders and two pipes, each about an inch and half in thickness and set apart by about two inches—and a top piece set across them, combining a pipe of about an inch and a half in diameter with one about two inches across. It looked something like a small, Dadaist metal sculpture of a tree. Brandon White Eagle coached Alan Washington, of the Chickasaw Nation's Department of Family Services, through the anxiety-ridden effort of bending the well-soaked end, tapered to about a quarter-inch thick, to form the first iteration of the cup. Washington's concentration radiated intensity, and for good reason. The job demanded an unusual combination of steadiness, strength, and delicacy. They began by determining the point of the apex for the cup and clamping it to the top of the broader pipe atop the metal tree with locking pliers. Once that was secured, the task of bending to form the cup started. Washington invested all the patience he owned—this was the point where Hamilton's earliest attempt at making kapochcha' came to grief. Although the wood was soaked and softened, it was by no means instantly pliable, and made noises threatening the sort of failure that already had sent a few blanks to the discard pile. After more than a minute of agonizing effort, he succeeded in bending the stick until the shoulder end came around the pipe to meet the handle. He and White Eagle worked quickly to apply a C-clamp to close the loop and form the throat of the stick.

Another stick, its cup already formed and clamped, rested with its loop around the top pipe of the four pieces under the part Washington just used, its handle resting at an angle on the girder just below. The intent was to allow the wood time to rest, as it must, to dry into and accept its shape, and to apply more, gentler stress to coax the cup to begin to flare.

Anyone who works with wood, especially if taken to such stress, will tell you time is the next tool to be called for. All successfully fashioned sticks were to have their clamps

A set of locking pliers holds the "cup" of a kapochcha' in progress in place on a stand made with pipe, much as a maker in the Homeland might use a tightly drawn and tied leather thong and a tree branch. Don't worry about the part peeling away from the right-hand side; the cup has yet to undergo much shaping and sanding.

Photo by Wakeah Vigil

Five sets of kapochcha' rest against the social-game goal post on the grounds of the Chickasaw Cultural Center in Sulphur, Oklahoma. The sets demonstrate the customization and variety of stickball sticks, ranging from lengths to types of wood, besides decoration and materials used for grip and protection.

Photo by Branden Hart

replaced by metal bands or sturdy cloth tape and then were set aside to await various finishing touches.

Many of the considerations involved in the final crafting are left to the all but limitless preferences of the players who use them. Some wind tape, whether plastic or cloth, around the parts of the handles they are most likely to grasp. Others favor the smooth touch of sanded and burnished wood. Customization can, and often does, go further. Ric Greenwood notes that players in Chikasha Toli might use different lengths of sticks, depending on the field positions where they usually play. For example, players in the team's defensive zone, nearest the goal they are charged to protect, may prefer sticks of full length because they offer the most obstruction against opponents' attempts and strategies to score. Longer sticks also help the player to throw the ball farther with less effort—in this case, upfield toward teammates closer to the opposite goal. Players stationed nearest the goal wherein they must score might use sticks cut shorter, the better to accommodate urgencies to quickly throw, pass, or shoot, especially amid the close and disruptive defenses they expect to deal with at that end of the field.

Hamilton prescribes that sticks, at their longest, should reach from the grip of the player's hand to the ground, basing that measure on the frequent need to scoop a ball up out of the grass, often while on the run. For an adult, that usually works out to about two and a half feet. At the revival of the traditional east-west game at Kullihoma, the sticks used by the players, when laid down during the significant solemnity of the pregame lineup and prayer, revealed a variety of lengths, from regulation—if we regard Hamilton's informal prescription as such—to at least one pair cut to perhaps less than a couple of feet long. The variation also demonstrated differences in styles and philosophies of play and more often indicated assignments of positioning on the

Photo by Branden Hart

field, as discussed above.

Even subtler customizations are popular, often for practical reasons. The crossed webbing inside the cup can be attached in different ways, according to the player's strategic preference. A right-handed player, Hamilton explains, might attach the longitudinal course of the webbing to the back of the cup of the stick held in the left hand, so to maximize its depth for catching or scooping the to'wa', something like the pockets that baseball players often toil to create in the palms of their leather mitts. The same end of the webbing might be attached to the front of the apex of the cup in the right-hand, or throwing stick, thus creating a shallower pocket for the ball, making it less likely to become wedged in the cup and easier to throw. Players most often stationed in the zone of the goal where they seek to score might attach the webbing of both sticks in the latter manner, meaning they can use either hand to shoot for goals.

The to'wa', the other most recognizable item of stickball equipment, has undergone some changes since the days of the examples found in the NMAI collection. Today's ball most often used in games played by the coed Chikasha Bak Bak and Chikasha Toli teams usually is, at heart, a golf ball, its trademark white dimpled exterior hidden under a cover wound in basket-weave fashion with leather lacing or "paracord," the narrow elastic nylon kernmantle rope (made as a set of smaller woven lines passing within a similar, slightly larger sleeve, sort of like its bulkier cousin, the bungee cord). Its name is a shorthand for "parachute cord," because it was primarily developed for that purpose and quickly became enlisted for a burgeoning number of other uses, especially arts and crafts. Some players also use it for lashing and webbing for their kapochcha'.

The result is a ball that weighs more and travels farther airborne than any made like, for instance, the specimens Hinson saw and detailed at NMAI. The balls in the museum

Three examples of to'wa' wound with woven paracord. Golf balls are often—but not always—used as the cores for such to'wa'.

are of traditional craft, with centers made of tightly packed animal hair, such as that of a horse or a deer, covered with a thin outer layer of leather stitched in a style reminiscent of, but ultimately unlike a baseball. In notes included in the book, *Chikasha,* Hinson recorded the circumference of one such to'wa' at five and one-eighths inches, only a bit smaller than a golf ball, although desiccation and time might have caused slight shrinking.

Even a newly made to'wa' of traditional manufacture and design would introduce broad variances between the fundamental characters of traditional and modern games. Ric Greenwood noted that his brother and fellow Chikasha Toli player Brad Greenwood took part in a traditional game among players of the Creek Nation in 2015 and reported to him that their ball, crafted more closely to the fashion of the ancients, tended to sail more and bounce less. Most notably, its lack of weight cost it the momentum necessary to cover distance like a golf ball-centered to'wa'.

"[It] is significantly lighter than the one used in the sport," Brad Greenwood said. "I can throw those balls from one end of the field to the other. The traditional ball—no matter how far you can throw—will only make it to the next section. So it has to be fought for all the way down to the other end." He observed during play that "while it's down on one end, there's a lot more resting [at the other end of the field]. But when it's near you, it stays near you."

He added that the ball used in that traditional game also had a "tail" on it, which inhibits flight. Such tails were seen among balls used during games of the past, and older examples of some similarly crafted can be found in museum exhibits. It is reasonable to believe that Chickasaw players of past traditional games used balls with such tails that could have been—and still can be—made from strips, tufts, or lengths of cloth, twine, or yarn, or sometimes feathers. In any case, as Brad Greenwood noted, the addition of a tail

Some to'li' players have managed to amass impressive collections of kapochcha' and regalia and have fashioned accessories like carrying bags that, although perhaps not strictly traditional, are crafted with respect to the culture of the Chickasaw past.

Photo by Branden Hart

effectively increases the surface of the projectile and keeps the to'wa' from spinning like balls in flight are wont to do. All of that in turn increases its drag, the mathematical concern of friction and resistance all flying things encounter. For the same reason, a tail further subjects the lighter traditional to'wa' to vagaries of the wind.

Most significant, however, is his instructive observation that "It's a fight the whole time with a traditional ball." With that we are returned squarely to the realm of Chickasaw warfare and its intimidating fury of sustained, pitched battles, often to surpass physical exhaustion. Descriptions of warlike spectacles set down, whether in oils or prose, by the likes of Catlin, Adair, the French officer Martin Bossu, and Horatio Bardwell Cushman, come to life at the imagination of a game in which the object, the to'wa', flutters and flips for fitful intervals, rather than rocketing downfield for distances. Whereas the modern game—the "sport," as Brad Greenwood distinguishes it—is a chase punctuated by skirmishes for the ball, the traditional to'li' is, unapologetically, a war waged for dominance of the field, foot by foot.

In that manner, the iron link between Chikasha to'li' and tanap (war) is forged to a greater strength in our understanding, through the regalia and equipment of the warriors who played and play the game.

A to'wa', wound basket-weave style with paracord, rests in the grass. The average ball for to'li' is about the same size as a golf ball.

Photo by Gentry Fisher

SECTION THREE
RULES
AND
REGULATIONS

A stickball official retrieves a to'wa' that has gone out of bounds at a game between Chikasha Toli and a team from the Choctaw Nation. Most often the ball or a replacement is immediately returned to action, without regard to which team had possession when it left the field of play.

Photo by Branden Hart

This account and description of Chikasha to'li' was written amid interesting athletic times. The institutions and authorities of presently the most popular sport in North American culture had only begun to feel effects of disturbing discoveries indicating its deleterious effects on the health—in sobering fact, on mental constitutions—of many men who earned great sums for performing football's more violent feats with crowd-quickening abandon. Not coincidentally, at perhaps no previous time was greater attention paid to the safety and health of athletes, especially youths who teem about the fields and courts of recreational sports.

Equipment crafted to specifications established by close study, such as pads, helmets, gloves, shoes, and even certain kinds of specialty underwear, played an important role in personal athletic protection. But the most popular measures arose from concepts of safe and equal play, codified as so-called "official" rules or regulations. Many such codes originated or evolved during the present era, and rarely have administrative structures of various sports hesitated to redress deficiencies found among them. Not long before this volume went to press, the highest professional leagues of baseball modified a certain rule after instances in which a sort of contact—i.e., a baserunner detouring his slide into base to prevent a nearby infielder from helping to produce two outs (the popular "double play")—caused gruesome injuries that endangered some players' livelihoods. A few grumbles arose, mostly from so-called traditionalists. Still, the prevailing attitude among most organized sports and their fans favored protecting athletes from avoidable injury.

Into that atmosphere stepped the renaissance of Chikasha to'li', which has for most of its history held to one firm on-field rule, encoded like a gene into the flesh and blood of the game: No touching the ball. As to contact with other

Photo by Branden Hart

players, especially amid the fury of the traditional game, *c'est guerre* ("such is war"), as eighteenth-century French military officer Martin Bossu might have put it. Bossu, who wrote an account of Choctaws playing the two-stick game they called tollih during his eighteenth-century tour of duty in what would become the American South, noted,

> they push and throw each other down; …
> and thus they dispute it to each other recip-
> rocally, with such an ardour, that they some-
> times dislocate their shoulders by it. The
> players are never displeased; some old men,
> who assist at the play, become mediators,
> and determine, that the play is only intended
> as a recreation, and not as an opportunity
> of quarrelling. …
> After playing well on both sides all the day
> long, every one retires with his glory or
> shame, but without rancour, promising to
> play again another time as well as they can.

Pushing, throwing down, dislocated shoulders—all nightmares of parents of young athletes, even despite Bossu's regard for the Natives' exemplary sportsmanship. As for the pushing, etc., things could get worse, as James Adair wrote some years after Bossu sailed back to the Old World.

"Once, indeed, I saw some break the legs and arms of their opponents, by hurling them down, when on a descent, and running at full speed," the English trader wrote. However, like Bossu, he noted, "It is a very unusual thing to see them act spitefully in any sort of game, not even in this severe and tempting exercise." In fact,

> By education, precept, and custom, as well as
> strong example, they have learned to shew
> an external acquiescence in every thing that
> befalls them, either as to life or death. By this

means, they reckon it a scandal to the character of a steady warrior to let his temper be ruffled by any accidents,—their virtue they say, should prevent it. … [T]heir constancy, which they gain by custom, and their love of virtue, as the sure means of success, enable them to perform all their exercises, without failing in the least, be they ever so severe in the pursuit.

Adair points us not to a contrast, but rather a parallel between what invaders saw as abandon and what the present culture calls sportsmanlike behavior. Drawing from his long experience among especially the Chickasaw, he brings the subject to its point in the phrase "the character of a steady warrior" and gives us a valuable clue about Southeastern and Chickasaw culture. The custom of tribal expectation is encoded in traditions that not only serve the tribe but also the individual, and is the most direct path toward realizing the best in either. Chikasha to'li' was and is not about being just a player in only a game. It has always been vastly more, and its unspoken rules are among the essential principles of Chickasaw life.

Adaptability in the presence of cultural change is basic among those principles. The modern discipline of astrophysics, in its incipient past, was compelled to discard an idea that the universe was and would remain static. In the same manner, historians and even so-called traditionalists should abandon the notion that as the Chickasaws were found during the contact period—either by Hernando de Soto or the other invaders—so they always must have been and, as the inference goes among some, so they always should be, to be considered as traditional. However, even traditions change. In the vastness of the Chickasaw past, uncounted migrations swept across landscapes, civilizations rose and flourished and decayed and fell, warfare rampaged among and about them, and strange peoples came and went, all leaving lasting marks—some like tattoos, others like scars. And so the business of history continues. Therefore adaptability, as far as Chickasaws are concerned, is about living our tribal life and not merely reacting against sometimes alien challenges that time customarily brings.

Therefore, at present the Chickasaw Nation's teams of Chikasha Toli and Chikasha Bak Bak have indeed and in fact continued strictly within our traditions, accepting adaptations in the game for the sake of cultivating its rebirth and new growth, in ways that have instituted a few—and only a few—rules to add to to'li''s lone cardinal commandment against touching the ball with the hands.

FIELD OF PLAY

In the traditional east-west game, two goals stand apart at whatever distance the field allows, and usually according to agreement before play begins. Some observers of the contact period asserted that fields could cover vast distances of a mile or more. Boundaries, however, do not exist for the traditional version, so chalk lines are rarely drawn. The to'wa' remains "live" and playable anywhere it may fly or fall. The unstated principle is that the whole earth is the playing field—after all, why not?—although the goals may stand more or less within sight of each other.

The same boundless character holds for the social game, in which all activity and strategy focus on the single, centrally placed goal post.

For Chikasha Bak Bak and Chikasha Toli, fields are most usually adapted to templates supplied by either version of the two games called football. For both the pads-and-helmets version and the other, no-hands-and-round-ball game we call "soccer," the usual field, including its so-called end zones, covers from 110 to 120 yards in length and 53 1/3 yards (160 feet) in width. The fields, if not already bounded by chalk or paint, are often marked to indicate boundaries beyond which a ball is no longer playable. Any to'wa' that leaves the boundaries is immediately replaced by a referee with a throw back onto the field from as near as possible to the exit point, and the teams must contest for the ball in that case—there is no restoration of possession.

GOAL SETTING

Because there are no boundaries in the traditional game, its goals usually only need to be equal in size and set opposite according to the agreed distance between them. They somewhat resemble the old-style, two-posted "crossbar" goals of pads-and-helmets football, albeit far smaller and narrower, often constructed from sapling trunks no more than about three inches in diameter. The posts of goals at the revival of the traditional game played mostly by members of Chikasha Toli in May 2015 at Kulliho-ma stood about six feet apart and rose to about nine feet from field level, with the crossbar lashed about eight feet off the ground. Players could score by "shooting" the to'wa' through the opening under the crossbar and between the posts or by carrying it clasped in their sticks through the same opening, so long as the ball did not touch the ground on its way. For example, a goal would be disallowed if the to'wa', being shot, bounced off the ground before continuing through the opening.

In the social game, the single goal post rises to as

A player shoots the to'wa' toward the effigy atop the social-game pole at the Chickasaw Cultural Center. Note how the defender has crossed his hands in an effort to deflect the shot. The effigy at the very top of the goal post—which can be any appropriate symbol; in this case, a fish—accounts for a difference in the rules of the social stickball game. To throw the ball against the goal post, without bouncing it, scores one point, while striking the effigy usually counts for two.

Photo by Branden Hart

Photo by Branden Hart

tall as thirty feet, and is often topped either with a carved wooden effigy, usually of a fish or a bird, or a simple plank perhaps a couple of feet long, set transversely across the tip. Two scoring levels may be offered, provided agreement beforehand. If so, striking the post with a ball either shot by a male player using sticks or thrown by a female player—making the social game the only version that allows any player to touch the to'wa' with the hands—counts for one point, while bouncing it off the effigy or plank set at the top of the post may count for two.

As in the traditional game, two opposite goals are used by Chikasha Toli and Chikasha Bak Bak, although each is a single post four inches square and about twelve feet tall. Current regulations dictate the goal posts should stand about eighty yards apart, with about ten yards of playable field behind each (see diagram, page 101). For youth games only, each post is circumscribed by a chalk or painted ring of ten-foot radius, suggestive of the "crease" set down in soccer and other field sports that feature broad, netted goals. Youth players may shoot for goals only from outside the circle. Therefore, unlike the adult Toli players, Bak Bak ball-carriers may not wade into the kinetic swarm of humanity guaranteed to be found around the goal. To do so would be to attempt the grimly named "suicide run," described in source material provided by Clovis Hamilton as an instance in which a single—and by rule, adult—player rushes the goal with the ball clasped in the sticks. By this strategy, a Toli player may try to score by reaching the post and tapping it with the sticks, provided the ball remains in firm possession. Conditions may be added in that instance. The rules for a coed tournament in 2014 during the Chickasaw Nation Annual Meeting and Festival stated that players who score in that manner must hold the ball in their sticks after they are "released from the pole for [one to three seconds]." The range perhaps allows for a referee's discretion, but it also

Players from the Tvshka Homma team of the Choctaw Nation defend their goal against a bid to score by Chikasha Toli. Note the defender holding up crossed sticks, presenting the greatest amount of obstruction possible. Also note the Chickasaw player positioned near the goal, ready to act if the shot is deflected.

gives quick-minded defenders a brief opportunity to foil the goal after the tap. Otherwise, and more often, players try to score by the more classic method of shooting, using at least one stick to throw the ball to strike the post. Toli players, of course, may shoot from any distance. A goal counts for one point in any case.

ROLL CALL

Invader observers of traditional games of past centuries at times veered into hyperbole when it came to their estimates of the number of players on field, often because they failed to consider conditions. George Catlin's panoramic three-part depiction of a Choctaw game, held soon after the arrival of the bulk of the tribe into Indian Territory circa 1834, suggests a vast contest. Thomas Vennum's research into Catlin's visit to the Choctaws, however, turned up evidence to suggest the event was staged as more a pageant than a game, combining an outsized demonstration with an example of the Choctaws' interest and involvement in their tollih. Thus the Choctaws humored the lawyer-turned-artist from the citified East. Adair, Cushman, Bossu, and others certainly mentioned instances equaling or exceeding Catlin's scale, often as part of annual customs, like the Chickasaws' Green Corn Ceremony. Still, it seems clear from their overall record that ball plays were frequently far smaller, especially when it came to the number of players. Team sizes for the traditional game, therefore, can be flexible. For the Chickasaw Nation's revival of the traditional game in May 2015, twenty-six men came to the field, divided into even teams by one of to'li''s most solemn and meaningful customs. The ceremony, involving prayer over the players,

Players in the revival of the "east-west" traditional game of to'li' in May 2015 at Kullihoma pose after their game. Kneeling, from left, are: Sunhawk Hill, Nick Underwood, Tim Maxville, Myer Hickman, Jeremy Wallace, Chance Factor, Dale Shackleford, Bo Postoak, Michael Allen, Ric Greenwood, Randy Shackleford, and Jason Burwell. Standing, from left, are: Jesse Lindsey, Leerene Frazier, Boomer Factor, Randall Templeman, Jared Greenwood, Clovis Hamilton, Brad Deramus, Brandon White Eagle, Jonas Manley, Levi Hart, Michael Freeland, Jamin Blanchard, Brad Greenwood, Joshua Hinson, Tim Jefferson, Gerald Hart, and Eli Hickman.

Photo by Wakeah Vigil

An example of a properly executed tackle during the revival game at Kullihoma. Note how Myer Hickman (in the gray T-shirt) has dropped his sticks before tackling Randy Shackleford, who holds the to'wa' in the cups of his kapochcha'. Behind the two, Joshua Hinson closes in while Bo Postoak approaches from the right.

Photo by Wakeah Vigil

their sticks, the field, and the game, set the men standing opposite each other by team, sticks laid to point straight before each. As in the past, a tribal elder stepped between the ranks, taking account not only of the number, but also of the known or apparent qualities of each player, in the strict interest of equality. The game would not begin until the teams could be judged, sometimes after arbitrary adjustment, as even in every accountable regard.

By the greatest of contrasts, rosters of the social version, if it could be said to have them, are filled by open and often impromptu invitation—come one, come all, come now. The preferences of any more or less official organizers of such a game may or may not determine the composition and ratios of what seem to be teams, usually divided as male versus female, without regard for age, size, or skill. To consider such a dearth of specificity as a prime ingredient of a prolonged instance of boisterous and bewildering madness is to approach a fundamental understanding of the social game, insofar as that is possible.

No limits are set at present for rosters of either Chikasha Toli or Chikasha Bak Bak. However, rules applicable to specific games, in turn governed or affected by any number of circumstances, may set how many players are allowed on the field. An item in a list of guidelines for Chickasaw Nation stickball recommends the number of players on the field—again, respective to conditions of a particular game—as from twenty to twenty-five for Bak Bak and up to thirty for Chikasha Toli. By that, the leaders of the Chickasaws' official teams indicated the recommended numbers of players for most competitions. In a reflection of the traditional game, much attention is given to equality of sides, at least with respect to number, although exceptions may occur. For the 2014 festival tournament, as an example, twenty-one players was established as an on-field limit in adult-level coed games, of whom five were required to be women. In an interesting turn, rules for the tournament noted that if any adult team could not send five women to the field, it could not use men as substitutes for them. Whether women could fill in for a shortage of men was not made clear. Should a team have fallen short of a full playing complement, the opposing team was given an option whether to match its number or play its full twenty-one.

CONTACT

The traditional version of to'li' presents us with the more squeamish accounts of the physical consequences of play. As noted before, the only standing rule for the traditional game sternly proscribes use of the hands to do anything with the ball during the game. The freewheeling nature and results of contact among its players, roundly accepted as a constant, is discussed elsewhere. However, the equanimity with which the player-warriors of the past dealt with the effects of such violence has seen itself progressively complemented of late by a cultural turn toward finesse and technique. From that arises terms for two types of disapproved intentional contact, i.e., hitting "early" and "late." To hit early is to tackle—in much the same impactful and restrictive method seen in pads-and-helmets football, only without the pads or helmets—another player before he or she has caught or otherwise secured the ball with at least one stick. To hit late, then, is to tackle a player after he or she releases the to'wa'. No penalty is codified for either in the traditional game, although the acts are looked down upon as marks of unskilled or poorly coached play, even if the offender obeys tradition by dropping his sticks before tackling. Grasping an opponent to restrict the use of his sticks is regarded fair play, but again, there is a proper way to do it, quite different from tackling. One should keep the sticks—both, in fact—in one hand while grasping an opponent's arm or sticks with the other. Use of the sticks to strike another player risks ejection from a game, but more as a consideration of propriety than enforcement of a documented rule. Such regards reflect growing appreciation among to'li"'s athletes for the game's best practices of ball-handling, speed, skill, teamwork, and scoring. Contact therefore is considered necessary only in certain instances, and players are expected to execute each instance properly.

In the social game, contact is routinely governed by a shared regard for the different ages, genders, and skills of players involved. The participant should expect at least the same kinds of contact one finds in a game of, say, backyard touch football or driveway basketball. Peculiar to the social game also is the dispensation for female players that allows them to use their hands to catch, carry, and throw the to'wa'. That unique condition changes the nature of the game. Although no codified set of rules exist for the social version, accepted tradition forbids males, who must use sticks, from offering better than passive obstruction against females in any instance. Should a male run over or bump against a female, the prevailing notion is that he should do so only in pursuit of the ball, and contact at least should appear incidental. Females, meanwhile, are bound only by common regard for decency and their inconvenient lack of immunity to applicable statutes of criminal and civil law. They may, as in the traditional game, seize the sticks of male opponents although, of course, they may use both hands. A common scene at a social stickball game, then, is one of a knot of male players toiling with their sticks to scoop a recalcitrant to'wa' out of the grass, only to suffer frustration when a female swoops in, knocks their sticks aside, snatches

A photo from a social game of stickball at Kullihoma, the Chickasaw gathering grounds about ten miles east of Ada, Oklahoma. Note the female player carries the ball in her hand, according to the tradition of the social game. Especially note the smiles on the faces of both players. The social game can be spirited, but it is seldom taken seriously.

Photo by Branden Hart

up the ball and flees, leaving them no recourse other than to chase after.

The modern game played by Chikasha Bak Bak and Chikasha Toli, for the present, holds the most definite rules in Chickasaw stickball to deal with physical contact. The presence of female players in both teams, and youth in Bak Bak, are important factors in their consideration and formulation. Infractions include the early and late hits discussed above, among a list of fouls common to many so-called contact sports, such as clotheslining (tackling by the neck), or striking another player intentionally with sticks, a foul similar to "slashing" in ice hockey. A list of rules for the festival adult coed game of 2014 included more points concerning contact:

- men only could tackle other men;
- women could tackle any other players;
- men could "check" (i.e., obstruct by brief contact) or bump women, although they risked ejection if a referee judged their acts as excessive;
- for men, the action of grabbing a female players' sticks or arms was restricted to the elbows downward;
- running into a "scrum"—a close knot of contending players, usually fighting for the to'wa'—or shoving another player into one was listed as a foul;
- players were forbidden to hit below the knees, tackle above the shoulders, target other players for physical contact unrelated to the game, "body slam" other players, or hit any player not in possession of the to'wa';
- however, the rules noted, any player without the to'wa' who yet succeeded in deceiving opponents into belief that she or he was in possession of it incurred the risk of contact without official pro-

Photo by Branden Hart

tection or recourse;

- players could (and often do) wear athletic shoes, but cleats of any kind were and are strictly prohibited;
- and, of course, fighting was expressly forbidden, and was the only foul severe enough to incur immediate disqualification from further participation in the tournament.

Rules for the Bak Bak youth coed team prohibit tackling, and checking may occur only between players of the same gender. Also for Bak Bak, a player may only seize an opponent's arms below the elbows, including the sticks. Referees counted most infractions in accumulations of three against individual players, with escalating penalties. The first compelled the guilty player to sit out for five minutes; the second, for the remainder of the half of play. A third commission of the same foul by the same player resulted in ejection from the game. The 2014 tournament rules for both age groups also codified a custom of the traditional game that dictates a combination of conditions in the case of tackling. In the first place, a player of any version of stickball may not tackle with sticks in hand. Doing so risks severe disapproval and perhaps worse in the traditional game, and rules of the modern version list it as an infraction. Also, should a player who has dropped his or her sticks to tackle one opponent then consider it necessary to tackle yet another, both the strict expectation of fair play in the traditional game and the written rule for the modern version intervene, stipulating the player must "reset," that is, return both sticks firmly to hand, which in turn means they must be dropped yet again before legally tackling the next opponent. The clearest intent is to keep players, whether one or many, from dashing stickless about the field with impunity, seeking whom they may tackle. The effective result is that the rule, written

Players from Chikasha Toli and the Choctaw Nation's Tvshka Homma leap either to catch or intercept a thrown pass during a game. Veteran stickball players master the skill of catching the ball with their sticks even while leaping into the air, as some are seen doing here.

The ball goes up, and the action begins at a game between the Chikasha Bak Bak team and young players of the Choctaw Nation. Note the official at left, tossing the ball upward.

Photo by Branden Hart

or otherwise, adds enough complexity to render tackling a bit too complicated for frequent use as a tactic and thereby regulates the amount of contact. Besides, one's opponent usually has passed or otherwise surrendered the to'wa' by the time a player who has just tackled another can reset. By that same token, the tradition and the rule combine to bring the players' focus toward skills and practices that call for more finesse, such as shooting, passing, stickhandling, and other finer pursuits and interests of the game. As for protective equipment, the rules set down by the Choctaw Nation's stickball league, of which Chikasha Bak Bak was a part at the time of this writing, required the plastic mouthpieces made to fit or mold to the player's teeth, popular among athletes who expect contact during play. Any youth players charged with protecting the goal, called goaltenders or goalies, also were required to wear protective helmets. Additional padding or protection was not prohibited by rule, but a ruling could be expected in any case where any equipment not ordinarily required might give a player or team an unfair advantage. Adult coed team members are not presently required to use protective equipment, although many use mouthpieces.

ADMINISTRATION & OFFICIATION

Observers noted the role of elders with regard to officiating and regulating the traditional game. At least many if not all elders so involved were former warrior-players, a status that sustained their judgments whenever technical controversies arose. It seems, from the records, their

A stickball official prepares young players from Chikasha Bak Bak and the Choctaw Nation for a game. Officials at such games are usually either adult players or former players, and well versed in the rules.

Photo by Branden Hart

most common contribution was the routine untangling of momentary complexities. As elsewhere discussed, they determined and enforced, by sheer authority, the equality of opposing teams. The number of such overseers was usually determined or agreed upon, often relative to the scale of the game. An elder would toss the ball upward to begin the game, somewhat like a basketball referee who lofts the jump ball. If the to'wa' somehow vanished or was destroyed, the elder would put a replacement into play. They certified or disallowed goals and kept official score. Most notably to the invader observers, they were the game's helmsmen, keeping all things at an even keel, so to speak, and taking firm control only when necessary, usually to steer players or spectators clear of ungovernable violence, if possible. Their standing as putative referees was at once as simple and intricate as their relationships to and within their tribe.

Much the same as the traditional game, officiating for the social version is customarily undertaken by elders or, if none are present, the nearest available Chickasaw adults with enough knowledge to judge the game, not to mention sufficient wisdom to decline to join in the chaos on the field. In whatever case, officials, as in the traditional version, judge the validity of goals and keep score. There may be squabbles—the game is too much of a free-for-all to determine whether fouls are committed, in most cases—and more experienced officials know well enough to render no judgment in disagreements bearing the whiff of personal grudges.

The nature of officiating at games played by the coed Chikasha Toli and Chikasha Bak Bak brings forth an important and fundamental point about stickball in the Chickasaw Nation. At least at the time of this writing, referees at their games underwent no certification beyond recognition and esteem of their experience and knowledge. The surrounding culture tends to prefer—in many cases, to insist upon—some accountable registration of responsibility, especially for oversight of a sport like stickball. Certain waivers and releases are signed before Chikasha Toli or Bak Bak players take the field, but that seems to be the closest we come to certification. The point of that should be a realization of the consistent cultural reliance of Chickasaws upon our community, and our community, in turn, on the constancy of our traditions. The strength of that reliance, in objective view, gives us a greater practical foundation than the predominant culture's dependence on the talisman of the official, which renders oversight of the game as something more like imposition by an external and vaguely impersonal presence. In practical terms, referees for Chikasha Toli and Bak Bak games are accountable for judgments concerning scoring and infractions discussed elsewhere, along with administrative matters like determination of equality of teams, quick return or replacement of balls gone out of bounds, and so on. Guidelines for Chickasaw stickball set no particular number for officials, in keeping with the variable numbers of players that may take the fields. The guidelines state that as many as twelve referees would be ideal for the average game, and that other nations may stipulate the number of officials for games they host. The 2014 coed tournament during the Chickasaw Nation Annual Meeting and Festival, as an example, called for six officials at either adult or youth games. An interesting addendum to rules touching officiating at that tournament directed participants to regard the festival's guiding committee as final authority in cases of dispute, a provision that again underscored the role of community in the administration of the game.

40 to 53.3 yards

circle at 10 feet in radius →

Offensive Zone

20 to 25 yards, +/−

110 to 120 yards

80 yards, +/−
between goal posts

Center Field

Defensive Zone

10 yards from goal post to out of bounds →

□ = GOAL POST

X = player (depicting one team only; positions are not fixed)

• dashed lines denote boundaries applicable only to youth teams
• all measurements are flexible depending on the field, etc.

FIELD POSITION

The usual progression of play in to'li', from one end to the center to the other end, provides a template for the field, dividing it more or less by thirds. The divisions may be delineated by markings or merely borne in mind, and how they are characterized is relative to each team. Attempts to score are made in the offensive zone; a second, transitory or pivotal zone in the middle is called center field; and the team must protect its goal in the third, defensive zone. The traditional game discards boundaries, so its zones exist only in concept, although an observer will see players remaining in positions that render them somewhat visible. Stubborn defenders and ball hawks work in the defensive zone, playmakers and deadeye passers patrol center field, and expert receivers and shooters play in the offensive zone.

In the social version, the single goal in the middle of the field collapses all zones into one. Every player must be instant to defend, relay, or score depending on where he or she happens to be relative to the goal and the peripatetic to'wa' at any time.

Field boundaries, as described elsewhere, are noted and marked for the modern version of the game as played by Chikasha Toli and Chikasha Bak Bak (see diagram, page 101). Lines also may be set down to describe the three zones discussed above, although they only apply as boundaries in the youth version. In an adult-level game, the number a team places in each zone depends on ever-changing tactical choices. Chickasaw stickball guidelines counsel only that players try to stay in assigned zones, for a considered reason. A team that vacates or leaves too few players in a zone effectively collapses its presence on the field. Such a tactical lapse offers the opponent the chance to control at least that zone and in some cases to score all but uncontested. For a youth-level game, inner field lines are more likely to be set down and can become barriers, often according to age. At the tournament in 2014 at Tishomingo, the younger group of players within teams, from eight to twelve years old, took responsibility for center field, although they were allowed to cross into either of the other two zones at their options. Elder players, from thirteen to seventeen years, were charged to remain in offensive or defensive zones, on pain of penalty—a warning at first for crossing into center field, followed by the calling of an infraction for a second instance, and ejection from the game upon further transgression. The area of center field usually covers at most twenty-five yards, depending on how much field is available and the preferences of the hosting team. Center field may be indicated by a chalk line or marker, or kept in mind as an agreed-upon spatial concept by officials who will issue necessary warnings or call infractions according to their judgments. Also, as noted elsewhere, another boundary pertains only to youth games—the circle setting a ten-foot radius around each goal post, marking the nearest point from which a player may shoot for a score.

MATTERS OF TIME

Accounts of the lengths of at least some traditionally played games of to'li''s past bear the whiff of legend. Some were said to have lasted for days, not unlike mass pitched battles waged over vast grounds. Descriptions of the conditioning and capabilities of Chickasaw warriors render such reports believable. They were known, like the fabled Zulu

A player for Tvshka Homma, a Choctaw Nation team, just misses an attempt to pick up the ball with his sticks while a Chikasha Toli player closes in during their game. The basic rule in all non-social organized stickball is the same: a player must always use the sticks to handle the ball—never the hands. Kicking the ball is also frowned upon.

Photo by Branden Hart

of the African plains, to run for long miles, and then immediately fight with such fury they hardly seemed the worse for travel. Often the duration was determined not by a measure of time passed, but rather by a negotiated number of goals to be scored in order for a team to be declared the winner. Traditional east-west games played in contemporary times may take up long periods, but usually not like those recorded from the past. The traditional game of May 2015 at Kullihoma was set to end at a certain time, but several minutes were added to resolve a tie score. Playing time therefore may be set by an agreed hour or kept as official, game-clock time, according to consent before the game begins.

The one-goal social version usually sets an agreed number of scores to declare a winning team and thus govern the length of a game. That determination, of course, may be affected by the time of day, how many players gather to join, or any number of other considerations (e.g., weather), all subject to agreement.

Games played by Chikasha Toli and Bak Bak can occur on fields belonging to other tribes who hold to other traditions and rules. Thus it becomes each host's responsibility to determine the length of the game, divisions of period play (e.g., quarters and/or halves), and official clock-keeping. As an example, rules during the festival tournament of 2014 established that each game be played by halves and added distinctions of length between games played at the beginning or in the winners' bracket—set at twenty minutes per half—or the losers' bracket, at eighteen minutes per half. The difference may have been instituted with an eye toward the amount of time available to complete the tournament. However, the Bak Bak team more commonly plays according to Choctaw youth stickball rules that establish eight-minute quarters for senior youth players and seven-minute quarters for juniors. In the case of a tie, one extra period can be played, usually limited to four minutes, although it ends with the first goal to break the tie. Also, as in some other youth team sports, a mercy rule may be brought into effect, according to guidance from Bak Bak coach Clovis Hamilton. If a team leads its opponent by an agreed number of goals—usually seven—after the end of the third period, the game is often called at that point, he said.

SUCCESS IS IN SHOWING UP

Most organized team sports, especially those so popular their best athletes might play them as professionals, bear the mark of standards, notably among players. Basketball players are generally quite tall and lithe. Pads-and-helmets football players range in size and bulk according to their positions, although larger than average men seem preferred overall. That such standards hardly darken the doorway of consideration for stickball should not come as a surprise to anyone with better than cursory acquaintance with the game. Any team of contemporary players of the two-stick game includes every size and shape, and no firm standard appears evident.

Styles and methods of play are also individual concerns. In contrast, baseball's hierarchies of skill rest on the levels of each player's mastery of its several tasks, although one player's techniques can seem much like another's, even if results often differ. Also, much of baseball's technical character is traceable to its status as a heavily institutionalized sport, with a history of evolution as a game and a culture that others often seek to emulate.

To'li' comes from a much different place and likely will never stray. The invaders' expropriation of the one-stick game, subsequently rebranded as lacrosse, almost robbed the Iroquois of a birthright and persists in Native minds as a cautionary example. And, too, it can be argued that for all the talent one might find on the field during the game, success tends to rely at least as much on field awareness, quickness, opportunism, or other matters of instinct, or even luck, as it does on discipline and technique.

At least a few techniques are recognized in practice, however. Prominent among them is the challenging task of learning to catch the to'wa' in flight—and often at speed—with the kapochcha'. Clovis Hamilton begins to teach the principles of that skill to new Bak Bak players with a simple introduction to the sticks.

A proper grip puts the handle within the fingers, a technique standard in baseball, golf, tennis, lacrosse, hockey, etc. To clasp the handle within the palm wraps the fingers too far around it, and thus involuntarily over-tightens the grip, which in turn renders the wrist less supple, and restricts the flexibility needed to properly wield the kapochcha'.

Hamilton takes new players to the basic task of learning not so much how to use the sticks as about them. He has them hold the one they usually catch or carry the to'wa' within—in the left hand for a right-hander, and vice versa—out with the cup facing upward, and the other held straight skyward, its cup facing forward. He instructs the players then to bring the second stick down upon the first, and join the cups together. At that many discover a revelation, particularly if their pairs are well crafted. The cups will fit together, with the "shoulders" facing outside, while the players' hands will line up more or less parallel at a comfortable distance. Younger players might repeat this act many times—as noted elsewhere, it mimics the snap of an

Ric Greenwood, left, and Clovis Hamilton are two of the leaders of the effort that has brought about the renaissance of stickball in the Chickasaw Nation. They also play the traditional Chikasha to'li', participate in and coach for the Chikasha Toli adult team, and coach youth for the Chikasha Bak Bak team.

Photo by Branden Hart

alligator's jaws. As simple as it seems, the practice introduces new players to their sticks in a way that tells them a lot, from how they should fit to how they should feel, and the flexibility they offer as extensions of their arms and hands.

From there players take on the responsibility to learn new and, at least at first, daunting tasks, such as catching the to'wa' in midair and shooting accurately. Hamilton and Ric Greenwood, among other coaches for Chikasha Toli and Chikasha Bak Bak, have learned the value of being both circumspect and intuitive in these regards, and respectful of one of to'li''s indelible traditional aspects, which accommodates individual approaches to the team-based game. Catching, throwing, and running may seem simple ideas. However, as we have seen throughout our study, to'li' turns such simplicities into complexities that demand either rigorous practice or the kind of talent that comes only from celestial origin. So, they are consistent in their counsel to players and any Chickasaws interested in playing that the most reliable, not to mention culturally responsible, way to cultivate success at to'li''s skills, particularly within the context of Chikasha Toli or Bak Bak, is to show up for practice.

BIBLIOGRAPHY

Adair, James. *The History of the American Indians.* 1775. Edited and with an introduction and
    annotations by Kathryn E. Holland Braund. Tuscaloosa: University of Alabama Press, 2005.

Bossu, Martin. *Travels Through That Part of North America Formerly Called Louisiana.* Translated from
    the French by John Reinhold Forster. London, 1771.

Busby, Orel. "Buffalo Valley: An Osage Hunting Ground." *Journal of Chickasaw History and Culture*
    10:1 (2004): 4-19.

Catlin, George. *Illustrations of the Manners, Customs and Condition of the North American Indians.*
    London: Chatto & Windus, 1876.

Cushman, Horatio Bardwell. *History of the Choctaw, Chickasaw and Natchez Indians.* 1899.

Dyson, John. "Chickasaw War Names and Four Homeland Colberts: William, George, Levi and
    Martin." *Ishtunowa: The Journal of Chickasaw History and Culture* 17:2 (Fall 2015): 6-21.

Hinson, (Lokosh) Joshua D. "To'li' Chikashsha Ịnaafokha: Chickasaw Stickball Regalia." Master's
    thesis. Albuquerque: University of New Mexico, 2007.

———— *Chikasha: The Chickasaw Collection at the National Museum of the American Indian.*
    Ada, Oklahoma: Chickasaw Press, 2014.

Humes, Jesse and Vinnie May (James) Humes. *A Concise Chickasaw Dictionary.* Edited by Lokosh
    (Joshua D. Hinson). Ada, Oklahoma: Chickasaw Press, 2015.

Lovegrove, Michael. *A Nation in Transition: Douglas Henry Johnston and the Chickasaws, 1898-1939.*
    Ada, Oklahoma: Chickasaw Press, 2009.

Morgan, Phillip Carroll. *Chickasaw Renaissance.* Ada, Oklahoma: Chickasaw Press, 2010.

Munro, Pamela and Catherine Willmond. *Chikashshanompaat Holisso Toba'chi: Chickasaw: An
    Analytical Dictionary.* Norman: University of Oklahoma Press, 1994.

Nelson, Stanley. "Play It Forward: Chickasaw stickball looks ahead to its past." *Chokma: Chickasaw
    Magazine* (Spring 2016): 22-31.

Perry, Robert. "Struggles for the Ball: Searching for the Game of Stickball from George Catlin to
    Modern Times." *Journal of Chickasaw History and Culture* 10:1 (2004): 20-28.

Swanton, John R. *The Indians of the Southeastern United States.* Washington, D.C.: Smithsonian
    Institution, 1979 (repr.).

Vennum, Thomas. *American Indian Lacrosse: Little Brother of War.* Baltimore: Johns Hopkins University
    Press, 2008.

Provided by Chickasaw Nation's Division of History and Culture, Department of Culture
and Humanities:

- Rules and regulations for Chikasha Bak Bak
- A template for a Chickasaw stickball handbook
- Rules for adult and youth participation in a stickball tournament held during the 2014
  Chickasaw Nation Annual Meeting and Festival in Tishomingo, Oklahoma.